FINDING STABILITY IN UNCERTAIN TIMES

SOME THINGS THAT HOLD FIRM WHEN EVERYTHING SEEMS TO BE FALLING APART

RONALD HIGDON

Energion Publications
Gonzalez, FL
2020

Cover Design: Henry Neufeld
Cover Image: Adobe Stock #329333231

ISBN: 978-1-63199-466-1
eISBN: 978-1-63199-467-8

Energion Publications
P. O. Box 841
Gonzalez, FL 32560

850-525-3916
energion.com
pubs@energion.com

Acknowledgment

My deep appreciation to Dr. John Lloyd who took the time to review the manuscript and make helpful notes and invaluable suggestions. I only wish I could have incorporated all of his "just a thought" observations into the text. They will certainly go into my file for future use. Many thanks to John for his deep insights, but most of all for his friendship.

DEDICATION

This book is dedicated to the many teachers, mentors, and friends who through the years have contributed to my thinking, re-thinking, exploring, deliberation, and shaping of the many on-going conclusions that undergird my life and faith.

TABLE OF CONTENTS

The time does seem to be out of joint.

Hamlet is certainly not the only one ever to call the time out of joint, to cry that the intended order of things was not running true to course. The recent appearance of books decrying the possible collapse of so much that we have taken for granted must mean there is an audience of those who feel the same way.

Perhaps it is time to reissue Paul Tillich's classic work from the '70s, *The Shaking of the Foundations.* Many confess that is an apt description of our current situation which Tillich found over half a century ago in Psalm 82. Verse five declares: *They have neither knowledge nor understanding, they walk around in darkness; all the foundations of the earth are shaken.*

The questions are obvious: Is there some knowledge, is there a place of partial understanding, is there at least a glimmer of light to provide some stability and security in such a threatening world? That is what this book seeks to provide.

This is not a book of shocking revelations.

If you want to get market attention, one way to do it is to write the most outrageous book one can imagine. After over sixty years of pastoral ministry, mine would be titled: *Why I No Longer Believe What I Have Been Preaching and Teaching All My Life.* This is *not* what this book is about. It is not about a loss of faith or an attack on what is wrong with so much in and outside the world of faith. One of the things I have learned (through years of practice) is that after the ranting and the raving something else must follow. This book represents for me that something else.

That something else is rooted in my biblical and religious heritage that always provided some clear markers. Not so much destination markers as direction markers like God's word to Abraham, "Go in this direction." Directional markers are not the same as "answer" posts, many of which I found to be detours in my faith journey. This is the reason for my underlying complaint: too many in too many fields of endeavor want to have things nailed down with the hammer blow of conviction that proclaims: "This is a settled issue." My chief complaint in the religious world is that too often those who have things nailed down will nail you down if you don't come to the same finalities they have reached. Whatever happened to the biblical reminder in 1 Corinthians 13: *We know in part?* Where is the recognition of that incompleteness that is forever part of our search for truth and wisdom? Where is that humility that confesses even after our best efforts our knowledge always falls short of the completeness that belongs only to God?

Although Paul maintains: *Now we see things imperfectly as in a poor mirror* (1 Corinthians 13:12, NLT), his writings assert there are some things we do see. Our imperfect vision does not mean total blindness. There is much that can be known but never with completeness and finality that sadly results in no further exploration or openness to greater dimensions of truth.

"Fixity is not a quality of serious reality."

The history of ideas and understanding quickly reveals that at many times and in many places many were convinced they had discovered the final piece in a particular puzzle of knowledge until only shortly thereafter other explorers found a different piece that made it necessary to give the former one a toss. Not so long ago it was a scientific "fact" that our earth was the center of the universe. The list of "we used to believe but now we know that…" is practically endless. Walter Brueggemann in *An Unsettling God* puts the idea like this:

> …fixity is not a quality of serious reality.…it is in process and in on-going transformation. When we are freed from static categories of interpretation that are widely utilized among us, we are able to see that the articulation of God in the Old Testament partakes exactly of the qualities of complexity, dynamism, and fluidity that belong to the post-modern world.[1]

Where we will travel in this book:

1. The world and the life of faith both loom larger with mystery. The immensity of everything is beyond our comprehension. To know this is to stand in the place of awareness.
2. We are not given all the answers we would like to have but more often than not we are pointed in a direction or given a way to proceed even with unanswered questions.
3. Ecclesiastes, after enumerating the things that do not bring meaning or purpose to our brief lives, concludes with the affirmation of an accountability day, affirming that who we are and what we do matter eternally to God.
4. Just as Jesus never gave his students (disciples) a diploma, even so we are enrolled in his life-course which I firmly believe continues into the life beyond.
5. Our common humanity enables us to live with compassion and empathy in a world where we literally are "all in this thing together."

---

1 Walter Brueggemann, *An Unsettling God* (Minneapolis: Fortress Press, 2009), xii.

6. The test of our life philosophies comes when we find ourselves at wit's end and need to rely on resources that are above and beyond any "self-help".

7. Imperfection appears to be built into our very existence and is the great reminder that there will always be many things we need to complete.

8. Forgiveness is the daily remedy for the healing of our relationships with God, others, and ourselves.

9. The world (life lived apart from God and his purposes) continues to keep shouting its principles while the voice of God's Spirit continues the whispers of wisdom.

10. Doubt and discouragement should never lead us to believe that God only responds to those who have perfect faith.

11. Every commandment in Scripture has to do with relationship in one form or another. It is these relationships that form the basis of our lives (both physically and spiritually).

12. Anger and fear will never lead us where we need to go; they are red flags that call for a deep examination of what lies behind them.

13. Living effectively in this world calls for the abandonment of the search for the peace and tranquility of any fabled Shangri-La.

14. Whatever can happen to anybody in life can happen to us — but not without God's abiding presence and unconditional love around us.

15. Whatever term we choose to use, it is evident that there are forces of evil present in the world that are contrary to the will and purpose of God. They may have their day, but they will have no part in God's eternity.

16. Understanding ourselves and others is practically impossible because the many deep secrets within all of us are well hidden.

17. The overarching theme of Scripture is the same from Genesis to Revelation: the unearned grace of God keeps pursuing us with his goodness and mercy (Psalm 23:6).

18. Change is built into the very existence of the universe. Dealing with these changes demands our openness to the leadership of the Spirit and responses that are prayerful, thoughtful, and reflective.
19. The crash at the end of the Sermon on the Mount is the great reminder that wishing, hoping, intending, and dreaming must all finally take back seats to a plan of action.
20. Not every decision needs to be made right now. Some require more space, information, or counsel until we have enough light to move forward.
21. *...no eye has seen, nor ear heard, nor the human heart conceived, what God has prepared for those who love him* (1 Corinthians 2:9).

Each chapter begins with a general discussion of the subject, followed by "Musings and Insights from Hither and Yon" in which I have the opportunity to explore some additional ideas that have been whirling around in my brain and lying dormant in my files. Each chapter concludes with "Questions for Reflection and Conversation." The Bibliography of Quoted Sources follows the Conclusion.

Let's sit down together and talk a little.

A word about my style of writing in this book. A friend who read one of my books made the comment, "I can hear your voice as I read." There continues to be some debate over whether or not there are two kinds of writing: one for reading and one to be heard. I always attempt to write for the ear as well as the eye. I imagine my reader seated across from me as I talk about things that matter to me in my life and in my faith. My goal is for maximum understanding, not for maximum agreement.

I trust you will find your journey through these pages to be as exciting, challenging, and faith-enhancing as I did in the writing. Let me know. My email address is rbooks5000@aol.com.

Ron Higdon

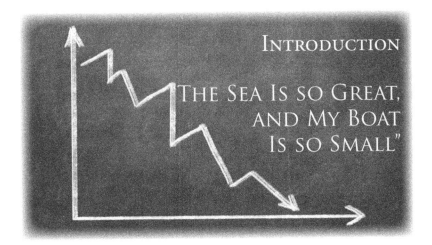

THE SEA IS SO GREAT, AND MY BOAT IS SO SMALL"

The above title is reported to be an old Breton fisherman's prayer. We don't have to be in the middle of a vast ocean to be overwhelmed by the magnitude of reality and the smallness of the vessel we are doing our best to keep afloat. When we were able to get men to the moon it was rightly hailed as a spectacular achievement. It was — until you consider what a speck that is in our solar system and how dwarfed that system is when placed in our galaxy and viewed from the perspective of galaxies beyond number that appear to stretch to infinity — and beyond. (The allusion to the movie *Toy Story* is intentional).

The sea used to be much smaller and our boat much larger.

We felt much more secure and things seemed much more predictable when we were the center of a system that was basically sun, moon, and stars. The discoveries of recent years, both telescopic and microscopic, have revealed worlds beyond the wildest imagination of even the best science fiction writers of the past. Vastness beyond vastness and complexity beyond complexity appear to be the order of creation.

As if this were not unsettling enough, add to this the complexity of each of us as human beings and you face another large mystery. We often complain that we do not understand another person. When I hear this, I want to ask (but never do), "Do you understand yourself?" In a Peanuts cartoon, Lucy gets to the heart of the matter as she stands at the blackboard and writes: "I will not talk in class." Frame two shows further writing of the same phrase. In frame three, Lucy pauses and appears to be in deep thought. Frame four has her writing: "On the other hand, who knows what I'll do?"

Even Paul in Romans 7 laments that he does not understand his own actions. He is perplexed by this ambiguity in his life. Some have attempted to relegate this chapter to his pre-conversion condition, but he seems to be speaking about the present and not about the past. He certainly describes my present-tense dilemma. Paul contradicts the philosophy that if people only know the right thing to do, they usually will do it. Well, not necessarily. There are always extenuating circumstances, peer pressure, other demands, risks involved — need I continue?

"Bleating" news seems to be coming from everywhere.

We have yet to touch on our awareness of the conflicts and chaos that continually erupt across the globe and come to us in living color, as they happen, through the courtesy of the ever-present "breaking news" outlets. Add social media that gives us much that only amplifies our stress in an overloaded information culture. In a movie of some years ago, one of the characters who has just received an alarming confession from the person seated next to him says, "Please feel free not to share that with me." That is one of my favorite quotes next to one in the same tenor where one person says in response to a rather too vivid piece of digestive information, "Why do I need to know that?"

In an era where almost everything seems to be overwhelming, the Breton fisherman's prayer takes on new meaning: the sea just keeps getting bigger and my boat just keeps getting smaller. This reflects the enormity of existence and our attempts to find some perspective or philosophy that will enable us to have a measure of control over the craft in which we find ourselves. Tom Butler-Bowdon put together two books that I couldn't resist adding to my collection. The first is *50 Self-Help Classics: 50 Inspirational Books to Transform Your Life (from timeless sages to contemporary gurus).*[2] The second is *50 Psychology Classics: Who We Are, How We Think, What We Do.*[3] These books reflect the many different approaches to understanding ourselves and our world. I have not been able to resist sprinkling some of this "wisdom" in the following chapters. Much is worth noting and pondering.

I'll tell you the secret and save you the read.

Some years ago, *The Secret* became a bestseller. (The secret is: whatever you send out is what you get back.) This was simply a new twist on Norman Vincent Peale's *The Power of Positive Thinking* (1952). Earlier versions of the same basic premise (cited in *50 Self-Help Classics)* include: *As a Man Thinketh* by James Allen (1902), *The Game of Life and How to Play It by Florence Scovell Shinn (1925); The Power of Your Subconscious Mind* by Joseph Murphy (1963); *Visualization by Shakti Gawaiun (1978)*; *Real Magic: Creating Miracles in Everyday Life* by Wayne Dyer (1992); *You Can Heal Your Life* by Louise Hay (1984); and *The Seven Spiritual Laws of Success by Deepak Chopra* (1994). Wonder why anything with this much coverage (which actually goes back much, much earlier in history) could be called a secret? (This usage of the term "secret" is in no way to be equated with a conundrum.)

There is no doubt that positive thinking, a positive attitude about life, and an emphasis on the good things in life are, to say the least, helpful and healthy attitudes. While this is true, the ques-

2   Tom Butler-Bowdon, *50 Self-Help Classics: 50 Inspirational Books to Transform Your Life* (New York: MJF Books, 2007).

3   Tom Butler-Bowdon, *50 Psychology Classics: Who We Are, How We Think, What We Do* (London: Nicholas Brealey Publishing, 2003).

tion is: "What else is also true?" I view with great suspicion any philosophy which proclaims, "All you need to do is…." Life is too complex and multi-layered for such a simplistic approach. In what we call *The Sermon on the Mount,* which I believe is a good summary of Jesus' teachings and what it means to live as Kingdom people, Jesus gives *many* things that need to be done in order to achieve the good life he came to bring.

MUSINGS AND INSIGHTS FROM HITHER AND YON.

There is not a single, simple explanation.

One of my recent highly recommended reads is *Behave: The Biology of Humans at our Best and Worst* by Robert M. Sapolsky. At almost eight hundred pages, it is a weighty and worthwhile exploration into the world of neuroscience. After in-depth discussions of many aspects of human behavior, in the epilogue Sapolsky makes this observation: "If you had to boil this book down to a single phrase, it would be: 'It's complicated.'"[4]

You would think that someone with this depth of knowledge would be able to give something a little more specific at the conclusion of his book. With all the research you might expect a genetic explanation for most of our behavior: "My genes made me do it." We will come back to this later, but I want to give this preview quote: "…while genes are important to this book's concerns, they're far less so than often thought."[5] (And as my reviewer pointed out: a major problem is that genes mutate).

The ocean of personal behavior is far deeper than we usually suspect, with many hidden factors coming into play. When Jesus asks the "possessed" man his name, he answers with a number: "Legion" (Mark 5:9). (A Roman Legion was about 600 men.) While *The Three Faces of Eve* was a movie that explored human complexity

---

4 Robert M. Sapolsky, *Behave: The Biology of Humans at our Best and Worst* (New York: Penguin Books, 2017), 674.

5 Ibid, 225.

and personality disorder, I suspect that most of us could supply some number for the numerous voices that attempt to influence our behavior. Paul is not the only one who ever cried, "I do not understand my own behavior!" (Romans 7:15 — my translation).

My take on all this: We are all far more complicated that we like to admit.

A pandora's box I won't open except for a quick peek inside!

There continues to be much discussion in certain theological circles about Divine Providence. Usually there is much name-calling and charges of heresy on both sides of such discussions. One of the best books I have found that presents clear arguments for both sides (Classical Theism and Open Theism) - without rock throwing — is: *Does God Have a Future: A Debate on Divine Providence* by Christopher A. Hall and John Sanders. This highly readable treatment found me underlining and starring much material from both sides of the argument. In an early chapter, Chris gives this much-needed reminder:

> James Packer taught me that biblical revelation…contains irresolvable tensions largely because God has chosen to keep certain things to himself, at least for the present…. Indeed, Moses taught Israel that the *"secret things belong to the Lord"* (Deuteronomy 29:29). Packer has warned me, both as his student in Vancouver and in many of his writings, to beware of draining the mystery out of the Scriptures in a misplaced desire for rational consistency."[6]

Even in making our way through the pages of Holy Scripture, it is necessary to remember that this sea seems to get even greater with our advancing years, and our craft of understanding (exegesis) frequently seems ever so small and in danger of being swamped.

---

6   Christopher A. Hall and John Sanders, *Does God Have a Future: A Debate on Divine Providence* (Grand Rapids: Baker Academic, 2003), 16.

QUESTIONS FOR REFLECTION AND CONVERSATION

1. In what ways have you found your sea getting greater and your boat getting smaller?
2. Have you ever wanted to respond to someone in this "Information Age": "Please feel free not to share that with me," or "Why do I need to know that"?
3. Did anything in the "Musings" section surprise or disturb you?

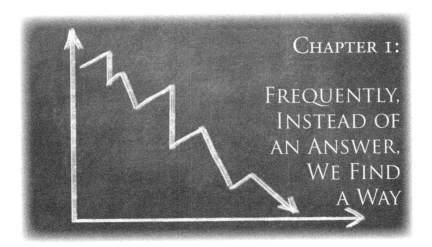

CHAPTER 1:

FREQUENTLY,
INSTEAD OF
AN ANSWER,
WE FIND
A WAY

The question that refuses to go away.

The cry of a heart broken mother in the movie *Steel Magnolias* is the perennial question: "If I just knew why!" Her plea is one I have heard in various ways from people (including myself) seeking answers to some seemingly senseless occurrence. The supposition is that if we could just find an answer then we would understand why such a terrible thing happened. Truth be told, there is no possible answer that would cause us to say, "Oh, now that I know why, everything is okay."

Not only is "why?" the most difficult question to answer, it is also the most useless question to ask. What difference will it make if someone tells us why? The situation of loss or tragedy will not be altered, the loved-one will not return, the situation will not be reversed. Nothing will bring back life to the way it was. The "why?" seeks a rational response to the irrational events in life. Almost all the whys I ask about life are dead ends. If anything, they only lead to more frustration and a deeper sense of helplessness in the face of life's assaults.

My classic illustration is found in John 9 and the disciples' question, "Why was this man born blind? Was it the result of his own sins of those of his parents?" (NLT). Except for saying, "Neither," Jesus did not supply a reason for a person being born blind. Instead, he said (my translation), "I will not give you an explanation but I will use this man's blindness as an occasion to demonstrate the grace of God." He gives this instruction, "*All of us must quickly carry out the tasks assigned to us by the one who sent me...*" (NLT) and then Jesus gives sight to the blind man.

What if the blind man could have been told: "Here is the reason you were born blind" — how would this have changed his condition? He would still have found it necessary to claim his regular roadside begging station every morning. This knowledge would have done nothing to enrich his life or lift his spirits. His blindness would have continued to be a reality. My interpretation of this event is, instead of seeking to know why a certain tragedy occurred, we are to seek a way — according to our abilities — to act creatively and redemptively in the situation. We are to be looking for a way instead of an answer. Note: that way is often not quickly or easily discovered.

The difference between an answer and a way.

It seems not accidental that the first Christians were called "Followers of the Way." Many have pointed out that Jesus did not say, "I am the answer." He taught: "I am the way." An answer is something you simply accept or reject. An answer is something you either believe or you don't believe. The Way is a path, a direction in life, a perspective you adopt, a journey you take, a commitment you make. To have a set of answers makes life too packaged and too small. It seems to imply that there is not much need for exploring, expanding, or asking new questions. It has always intrigued me that the rabbis (almost without exception) taught that the secret of life is not in the discovery of certain answers but in learning how to ask better questions. This is illustrated in the classic story is of the Jewish mother who greeted her son upon his return from school with: "Did you ask any good questions today?"

Living by answers is always in danger of becoming judgmental: if I have the answers, my only task is to convince you I am right. People march every day with banners proclaiming simplistic answers to complex questions. I always want to ask, "You may be right under certain circumstances, but is this the right answer under *all* circumstances?" The classic *Pilgrim's Progress* is the best argument for seeking a way rather than answers. As Pilgrim makes his way, the challenges and changes in life literally change him. This is what happens when you are a follower of the Way. It is not meant to make us Know-It-All Believers, but those who are growing in grace and knowledge (wisdom). Answers are frequently too excluding. Answers often leave too little room for a greater dimension of the truth and for different aspects of one's answer to be explored.

I have no doubt that I am called to be a consistent learner as I make my journey through the life of faith. Although there are indeed some answers I have found and some truths that have grown larger in my life, I am not called to be the Answer Man.

MUSING AND INSIGHTS FROM HITHER AND YON.

Many answers are simply not big enough.

It has always seemed to me that many of the answers I have heard have been not so much incorrect as they have been far too small. Then again, little questions call for little answers which is one of the reasons we need to keep making our questions bigger. We usually want to have answers in order to keep life manageable. We don't want words like mystery, paradox, and ambiguity (words I will keep using in this book) to interfere with our explanations. These words should be the continual reminder that the expanding sea of the unexplored make our small boats ill-equipped to ride out the increasing heights of the waves of the unknown.

A Surprising Place to Begin.

On her deathbed, Gertrude Stein is said to have asked, "What is the answer?" Then, after a long silence, "What is the question?" Don't start looking in the Bible for the answers it gives. Start by listening for the questions it asks.[7]

Buechner is not the only one to make this suggestion. I once did two sermon series: "Questions from the Hebrew Scriptures" and "Questions Jesus Asked." The Bible opens with what I call the two great questions (both asked by God): "Adam, where are you?" and "Cain where is your brother?" Of course, no single sermon could begin to address all of the dimensions found in each question. A case can be made for considering the remainder of Scripture the attempt to answer these two questions. I still believe the best Bible reading I do is when I allow it to question me. I still believe a better question than, "Have you read any good books lately?" is: "Have any good books read you lately?"

Much too frequently, I do not have sufficient understanding to be able to craft a question that will give me the answer I need. Some of Jesus' most surprising lessons come from his re-directing a question that is being asked. When he was asked, "Is it lawful to give tribute to Caesar or not?", he asked for a Roman coin and changed the question to: "Whose image is on this coin?" His "answer" to those who confronted him that day was, "Give to Caesar what belongs to Caesar and to God what belongs to God." In truth, he never answered the question! He gave a much larger question that called for reflection and discussion. He opened up a much larger world than the small question posed by his enemies.

---

7   Frederick Buechner, *Listening to Your Life* (New York: HarperSanFrancisco), 124.

Faith Unraveled: How a Girl Who Knew All the Answers Learned to Ask Questions.

The above is the title of a book by Rachel Held Evans. The book was first issued under the title *Evolving in Monkey Town*. Rachel Evans lives in Dayton, Tennessee, the scene of the "famous" Scopes trial. The trial was supposed to settle once and for all the battle between faith and science. Evans gives a brief, but fascinating read of what was described as "the trial of the century." More than two hundred reporters from as far away as London came for coverage during the summer of 1925. "People could pay to get their picture made with a live chimpanzee, and the town constable even put a sign on his motorcycle that read 'Monkeyville Police.'"[8]

Clarence Darrow and William Jennings Bryan put on quite a show which Evans describes. Her comment on the event: "These days most Christians, even conservative Christians, acknowledge that the Monkey Town approach of stubborn isolationism and anti-intellectualism is an outdated and ineffective strategy for expanding the kingdom."[9]

One of her most striking observations is: "The more committed we are to certain theological absolutes, the more likely we are to discount the work of the Spirit when it doesn't conform to our presuppositions."[10] A brief line on the back cover best describes what this book is all about: "How an evolving spiritual journey leads to an unshakable faith." It's not about a faith that remained unraveled but about a faith that found its way because of new and better questions.

---

8   Rachel Held Evans, *Faith Unraveled: How a Girl Who Knew All the Answers Learned to Ask Questions* (Grand Rapids: Zondervan, 2010), 53.

9   Ibid, 64.

10   Ibid, 155.

It's one of the reasons my reading has become very broad.

Listening to people espouse beliefs different from mine is informative, not threatening, because the only thing that can alter my worldview is a new and undeniable truth, and contrary to what Jack Nicholson says in *A Few Good Men*, "I *can* handle the truth."[11]

What I'm saying is not that the great truth was Parkinson's specifically, but that there are realities that occur in life over which I have no control or influence, realities that I can't negotiate, finesse, or charm.[12]

My reading has gotten much broader through the years because I faced "realities I couldn't negotiate, finesse, or charm" and found it necessary to listen to some other voices. My faith did not become unraveled, although the questions came thick and fast. In the end, my faith became richer, deeper, and truer to the biblical witness as my much too narrow vision was opened to new truths that did not so much shatter all the old ones as clarify and expand them.

The truth of the Way was much more profound than the truth of the simple answers that stood guard over my faith. I grew up in the same kind of religious environment as Rachel Evans and I know whereof she speaks. I will be forever grateful for the voices that brought me to questions I never dreamed existed and a Way that led to more comprehensive answers.

A recent find that illustrates the above idea.

While browsing in a used bookstore (some people still do this), I came across *The Jewish Annotated New Testament*. The Editors' Preface explains the reason for this book:[13]

---

11   Michael J. Fox, *Always Looking Up: The Adventures of an Incurable Optimist* (New York: Hyperion, 2009), 160.
12   Ibid, 180.

…Jews and Christians still misunderstand many of each other's texts and traditions. The landmark publication of this book…will serve to increase our knowledge of both our common histories and the reasons why we came to separate.

…in addition to emphasizing the Jewish background — or better, the Jewish contexts — of the New Testament, we pay special attention to the passages that negatively stereotype Jews or groups of Jews…..[13]

Jesus and Paul were both Jews who were faithful to their heritage and traditions; this book provides valuable insights into the Jewish world in which they lived and worked. I just completed reading *Common Errors Made About Early Judaism,* one of many excellent essays in the back of the book. It gives much-needed insight and correctives to our assumptions about the New Testament world. One that was not new to me is that there were many divisions within Judaism and no single belief in the role of the coming Messiah. Diversity marked the religious world of that time even as it marks the world of our time.

There is no better way to understand Judaism than to listen to Jewish writers talk about their faith.

QUESTIONS FOR REFLECTION AND CONVERSATION

1. Does my interpretation of the episode in John 9 make sense to you?
2. What do you understand to be the difference between an answer and a way?
3. Are you comfortable with the discussion about a broader base for reading?

---

13 Amy-Jill Levine and Marc Zvi Brettler, eds., *The Jewish Annotated New Testament* (New York: Oxford University Press, 1911), xii.

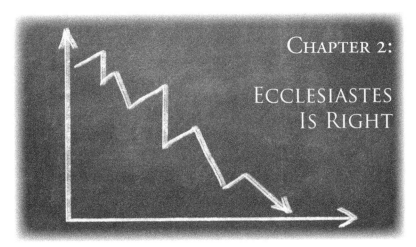

Chapter 2:

ECCLESIASTES IS RIGHT

THE TEACHER OFTEN SAYS THINGS WE DON'T WANT TO HEAR.

Ecclesiastes is ordinarily not one of the biblical books read for inspiration. It begins on quite a low note and never really seems to rise above its basic pessimism. The usual translation of verse two in chapter one is the teacher's lament: *Vanity of vanities — all is vanity.* My preferred translation is: *Meaninglessness! Meaninglessness!* (TNIV). This unnamed teacher then begins a catalogue of the many ways he has sought meaning for his life, including: pleasure, wisdom, riches, and hard work. His discourse is filled with much of what we would term "negative thinking" ending with: "What difference does anything make anyway? We all have the same destiny — the grave."

It is to be noted that, as one of the Wisdom books in the Hebrew Bible, Ecclesiastes does have much to offer. Who has not heard chapter three's familiar opening verse: *There is a time for everything, and a season for every activity under the heavens?* Following his list, most are surprised by verse eleven: *(God) has made everything beautiful in its time. He has also set eternity in the human heart.* Another widely-known verse is found in the opening of chapter seven: *A good name is better than fine perfume.* There are also some excellent proverbs in this chapter as well as the call for moderation in all things: *Do not be over-righteous, do not be over-wicked* (3:16-17). A large piece of wisdom which remains highly controversial will be discussed in chapter fourteen (9:11).

Aside from some memorable phrasing, the Teacher's conclusion has been the text for many sermons: *Now all has been heard; here is the conclusion of the matter: Fear God and keep his commandments, for this is the duty of every human being. For God will bring every deed into judgment, including every hidden thing, whether it is good or evil* (12:13-14). James Limburg gives this commentary:[14]

> "The end of the matter," says verse 13, and the book of Ecclesiastes comes to a close. As a good teacher…(he) summarizes the whole thing in just a few words, "while standing on one foot," as the rabbis liked to say: "Revere God, and keep God's commandments!"…And then says the Teacher, translating the Hebrew literally, "This is everything for humans." (Mine: The CEV translates: "This is what life is all about.")

There's a great day coming.

I find verse 13 to be a key in bringing meaning and purpose to life: it is the word of judgment; it is the word of accountability. Most of us remember that when a High School teacher made a reading recommendation not on the required list, someone would always ask, "Will this be on the final?" If the answer was, "No," the number who read the suggested book took a significant downturn. When we know we are accountable for everything then everything takes on new meaning. There *is* One who cares about what we do, about how we live. There *is* One to whom we are accountable. Our lives matter; we matter. Limburg informs us that Jewish tradition directs that in reading Ecclesiastes publicly, verse 13 should be repeated, so that everything ends on a positive note.[15]

---

14   James Limburg, *Encountering Ecclesiastes: A Book for Our Time* (Grand Rapids: William B. Eerdmans, 2008), 18.

15   Ibid.

You don't read Ecclesiastes like you read the book of Romans.

A good rule of thumb is that before you begin reading anything in the Bible, you find out what kind of literature you will be encountering. I remember how helpful it was to hear in my Old Testament survey class at seminary that the first eleven chapters of Genesis are often referred to as "The Theological Prolegomena" to the Hebrew Scriptures. They contain the stories that set the stage and provide the context for the history of the Hebrew people that begins in chapter twelve. You immediately sense a change in the nature of the text when you read: *Now God said to Abraham....* Thus begins the story of Abraham and his descendants which fills the next thirty-eight chapters of the book. You immediately notice the difference in the tone of the writing from what you encountered in the first eleven chapters.

Another quick illustration: you don't read the book of Job the same way you read the book of Romans and you don't read Romans the way you read Paul's other letters. To begin with, rather than a typical piece of correspondence written to a congregation in order to address questions or specific problems, Romans is more or less a theological treatise. It is the most carefully crafted of Paul's writings and is intended to be for congregations everywhere rather than just the church in Rome (which Paul had not visited). The book of Job, except for the brief Prologue and briefer Epilogue, is poetry. Most translations (except for a few like *The Jerusalem Bible)* do not reflect this in the way the text is laid out. This massive dose of poetry in a book labeled "wisdom literature" signals a different approach in reading and interpretation.

Biblical books in the category of "Wisdom Literature" include: Proverbs, Job, Ecclesiastes, and Song of Songs (sometimes listed as The Song of Solomon). These writings are about how to live in a world where challenges to faith abound and few signposts are provided. I give you a twist on something most of us have heard: "It's a shame we're *not* born with a set of instructions." But then again, this might make us robots and that is certainly not what it means to have been created in the image of God.

The wisdom books are intended for reflective and conversational reading. They are meant to be analyzed, discussed, and debated. They are not to be read in the same way you would read the historical portions of Scripture (which, of course, are always written from a faith perspective). Keep in mind: the rabbis taught that new meanings were to be discovered in Scripture for the current time in which it was being read. Their regard for the text is the same as mine: Scriptures are always deeper, richer, and more far-reaching than our current interpretations are able to deliver. In my re-reading of the Bible, I never cease to be amazed at how many new things I discover. It is the same text that has always been there, but I am not the same person I was at earlier readings.

MUSINGS FROM HITHER AND YON.

It does make sense after all.

> *In this meaningless life of mine I have seen both of these: the righteous perishing in their righteousness, and the wicked living long on their wickedness. Do not be over-righteous, neither be over-wise — why destroy yourself? Do not be overwicked, and do not be a fool — why die before your time? It is good to grasp the one and not let go of the other. Whoever fears God will avoid all extremes.* (Ecclesiastes 7:15-18).

Before you dismiss this idea, I ask if you can see any of this kind of moderation in the life and teaching of Jesus? The Pharisees were the super-righteous of their day and in their extremism missed the mercy and compassion that Jesus insisted were more important aspects of faith. It may be a little more difficult to mine the biblical wisdom in Ecclesiastes, but we should never lose sight of this: it is a part of Holy Scripture and it needs to be taken into account to receive a proper balance in our theology.

My broad readings often include a New York Times Bestseller simply because I want to be in touch with what a significant segment of the population is reading. One of those of a few years ago was *The Untethered Soul* by Michael A. Singer. My confession: I bought the book because of the subtitle: *The journey beyond yourself.* This is a large part of Jesus' teaching, and we have always had a difficult time incorporating it into a healthy spirituality.

Here is an excerpt from Singer's book in a chapter titled "The Secret of the Middle Way":

> No discussion of living life as a spiritual path is complete without addressing one of the deepest of all spiritual teachings, the *Tao te Ching*. It discusses that which is very difficult to discuss, that which is called "the Tao" (pronounced: dow). Literally translated, this means "the Way."[16]
>
> Those are the two extremes of the pendulum: the yin and the yang, expansion and contraction, non-doing and doing. Everything has two extremes. Everything has graduations of this pendulum swing. If you go to the extremes, you cannot survive.[17]

It's not a teaching that is a mainstay of our culture.

> Wendell Berry: "Don't own so much clutter that you will be relieved to see your house catch fire."[18]

This subject is so serious that I felt we needed to begin with a little comic relief to lighten the load. One of Jesus' clear teachings is that a person's life does not consist in the abundance of possessions that can be accumulated. Warnings against depending on "stuff" to bring satisfaction and happiness shouldn't need any

---

16 Michael A. Singer, *The Untethered Soul* (Oakland, CA: New Harbinger Publications, 2007), 165.

17 Ibid, 166.

18 Donald Altman, *Clearing Emotional Clutter* (New York: MJF Books, 2016), 1.

further proof than the testimonies of those for whom they have produced a meaningless life - like the Teacher of Ecclesiastes:

> *I denied myself nothing my eyes desired;*
> *I refused my heart no pleasure.*
> *My heart took delight in all my labor,*
> *And this was the reward for all my toil.*
>
> *Yet when I surveyed all that my hands had done*
> *and what I had toiled to achieve,*
> *everything was meaningless, a chasing after the wind;*
> *nothing was gained under the sun* (2:10-11).

Jesus never denigrated the wise use of possessions; many of his followers were people who were considered wealthy. Jesus taught never to equate bigger barns with bigger lives or with meaning and purpose. Our lives cannot be measured by the abundance of our possessions. I'll leave this hot potato for you to consult the Gospels for further enlightenment.

We Are Just Passing Through.

There is an old gospel song with the line: "This world is not my home, I'm just a passing through." The biblical description of who we are is repeatedly described as "pilgrim." A recurring theme in Ecclesiastes is that not much really matters because, after all, we all end up in the grave. That is the darkest theme in the book and it only tells a portion of the story — but it is a portion we ignore at our peril. We often fail to see life as gift and our brief journey here as a time to make the most of every hour that is offered to us.

And there is another thing to learn from this brevity:

> Why should anything that anyone says or does cause you to get disturbed? You're just on a planet spinning around the middle of absolutely nowhere. You came here to visit for a

handful of years and then you're going to leave. How can you live all stressed-out over everything? Don't do it.[19]

Brevity does not equal meaninglessness in the context of faith. We will address this issue more fully in the Conclusion, "Is This As Good As It Gets?"

QUESTIONS FOR REFLECTION AND DISCUSSION

1. Have you spent much time reading Ecclesiastes or the other Wisdom books? Why do you think this is so?
2. Do you believe in living the middle way?
3. What have you found that brings satisfaction, meaning, and a sense of purpose?

---

19 Michael A. Singer, *The Untethered Soul*, 135.

There is a better word than "disciple."

In a recent translation of the Gospels, I have found it most instructive that the Greek word usually rendered *disciples* now reads *students: And Jesus said to his students.* Too many current ideas about being Christian have to do with certain things that one believes. I concur that the Christian faith has content, but it is easy to forget that the earliest Christians were called "Followers of the Way." They believed that Jesus was the long-awaited Christ (Messiah) and confessed him as savior but that was only the beginning. That was step one. It was not Christianity full-blown.

It is unfortunate that one particular way to translate key verses in John 3 has tended to make conversion into a package transaction with the resultant, "Well, now I've done that." I'm talking about Jesus' command to Nicodemus: *"You must be born again."* I believe the much better translation (and one that fits far better into the entire conversation of the chapter) is: *You must be born from above; you must be born of the Spirit.* Although the first certainly implies the need for growth and learning, the second places conversion in the context of Kingdom ethics and the way of the Spirit. It gives direction and content to the kind of new beginning which "acceptance of Jesus as savior" involves.

The rabbi's lessons are never finished.

Jesus spent his earthly ministry teaching his students. The primary title for Jesus in the Gospels is Teacher. In the Sermon on the Mount, Matthew depicts Jesus as a rabbi with teaching authority when he tells us: *Now when Jesus saw the crowds, he went up a mountainside and sat down. His disciples came to him, and he began to teach them.* The Synagogue custom was for the rabbi to stand for the reading of Scripture and to be seated for his teaching. Matthew was also picturing Jesus as the new Moses (cf. Moses on Mount Sinai and Jesus on a mountainside).

Jesus never presented any graduation diplomas to his students. To the contrary, he constantly called them to task for so easily forgetting some of the earlier lessons in his curriculum. Even toward the very end of his earthly ministry they were arguing about which one of them was the greatest. His promise was that on his departure, the Spirit (Holy Spirit, His Spirit) would continue to teach and lead them into further truth. He never hinted there would be a time when school would be out. They were to be perpetual learners and discoverers of aspects of the life of faith they never knew existed.

I believe school is never out because we are consistently at a new age and level in life that causes us to be open to new truths and insights. Some complain they were never taught in seminary many of the things they found they needed when they began ministry. (The same probably holds true for all institutions of higher learning.) In my case, I believe most of these things were taught but I simply was not at the place in life where I could hear them. My life experiences were too few and the ups and downs of dealing with church congregations had not yet made me aware of how much there was yet to be learned. My learning continued, my library grew, and my acknowledgment of how little I really knew increased at an alarming rate. It soon became obvious I had a long way to go and I never anticipated a graduation date. The sea was too great and my boat was too small.

Unfortunately, there is something that not only rings the closing bell for classes, but robs us of what we already know.

I only wish that when I had written my last book, *Aging is Not Optional: How We Handle It Is*, that Tia Powell's *Dementia Reimagined* had been available. It was issued in 2019. In my section on Alzheimer's it would have been one of *my* must-read recommendations. I give you a few insights from that book simply to encourage you to a secure a copy for a thorough exploration of her subtitle: *Building a Life of Joy and Dignity from Beginning to End:*

> Dementia lasts for years. Most of that time, people with dementia retain the skills, memories, and passions that allow joy and inclusion in the larger social world, if we would but let them in.[20]

> …a great deal of what medicine offers patients is care… Yet medicine is too embarrassed to admit this. Care seems soft and unscientific: we'd prefer to hand out swashbuckling cure. It could have gone the other way. Medicine could have taken seriously the Hippocratic instructions to cure sometimes, treat often, comfort always.[21]
> A distinction needs to be made between dementia and Alzheimer's disease.[22]

> Powell gives an extended section on how to build "cognitive reserve" and its importance in protecting brain function. Much of it has to do with continued learning in many areas of life.[23]

---

20 Tia Powell, *Dementia Reimagined: Building a Life of Joy and Dignity from Beginning to End* (New York: Avery, 2019), 2.
21 Ibid, 5.
22 Ibid, 138.
23 Ibid, 156.

The insurance companies don't want your business. They are getting out of long-term care in droves.[24]

Today, thoughtful experts work to create dementia care that does not just kill time until death, but offers a way to live well.[25]

MUSINGS FROM HITHER AND YON

What is education (real learning) anyway?

Education has always been defined as the development of certain capacities (for example, critical thinking and the tolerance of ambiguity) that allow the educated person to live more productively and at peace in a complex and demanding world.[26]

The reason school is never out and we remain students all our lives is that learning is not a matter of simply coming to answers about the questions life offers. It means using critical thinking (in extremely short supply in the present culture) to enable us to find a way to live "in a complex, demanding, and ever-changing world."

Followers of the Way are those who are supposed to be able to see things in a different way, who have a new perspective on life and its difficulties. I thought the idea was an original one, but I have discovered that many others have made the same suggestion:

(In the second half of life) the Eight Beatitudes speak to you much more than the Ten Commandments now. I have always wondered why people never want to put a stone monument of the Eight Beatitudes on the courthouse lawn.[27]

24 Ibid, 172.
25 Ibid, 222.
26 Parker J. Palmer, *To Know As We Are Known* (New York: HarperSanFrancisco, 1993), xviii.
27 Richard Rohr, *Falling Upward: A Spirituality for the Two Halves of Life* (San Francisco: Jossey-Bass, 2011), 119.

My take on the answer to this question is that the Beatitudes are much more demanding than the list of commandments (in the original Hebrew known as "The Ten Words"). When you read Matthew 5-7 you quickly discover that Jesus' Way is much more than a list of rules; it is an entirely new way to see ourselves in this world and requires constant re-evaluation and critical thinking. School is never out when the Beatitudes become your directive for the Christian life.

This may be too much for some to take.

> Authentic spirituality wants to open us to truth — whatever truth may be, wherever truth may take us. Such a spirituality does not dictate where we must go, but trusts that any path walked with integrity will take us to a place of knowledge. Such a spirituality encourages us to welcome diversity and conflict, to tolerate ambiguity, and to embrace paradox. By this understanding, the spirituality of education is not about dictating ends. It is about examining and clarifying the inner sources of teaching and learning, ridding us of the toxins that poison our hearts and minds.[28]

Parker Palmer is one of my favorite authors — a Quaker who offers me a way to find many truths that give my faith new depth. He offers again those challenging words: diversity, conflict, ambiguity, paradox. I am convinced that any mature spirituality will embrace these words. The Pharisees Jesus had a problem with were those who had eliminated them from their faith-stance and had no room for anyone who colored outside the lines of their narrow orthodoxy. (It should be remembered that not all Pharisees rejected the teaching of Jesus.)

When Jesus announced he was the Way, the Truth, and the Life, it sent those who decided to follow him on a new path into the discovery of new truths — many times an enlargement of truths they already held. My seeking of truth wherever it might lead has

---

28 Parker Palmer, *To Know As We Are Known*, xi.

not brought me to a rejection of the basic tenants of my faith but an enlargement and flexibility that I did not find in my early church experience. Unfortunately, I now view that experience as one that was "signed, sealed, and delivered" with no tampering allowed. Certainly, no challenging questions allowed. If the goal is to eliminate diversity, conflict, ambiguity, and paradox from your faith it will mean a closing off to further exploration and discovery. Jesus' promise of the coming Holy Spirit (His Spirit, God's Spirit) was the promise of one who would lead into larger truth that at the time his disciples were not equipped to handle. Palmer's book describes just how challenging some of that new truth was as the Good News made its way into the Gentile world.

It remains a challenge for me to put these into daily practice.

> *Response* takes time, *reaction* is instantaneous.
> So, the trick is to raise your consciousness from the lowest to the highest level of awareness no matter what is going on around you. Remember, *reactions* are instinctive, *responses* are thought out. That is, thoughts pushed forward.[29]

Much too often in my pastoral experience, I found myself reacting instead of responding. I found myself getting on the defensive instead of listening to a complaint to discover if there might be something I needed to work on. Much of this reaction was based on some past experiences that had not been worked though. It is so much easier to react because no thinking is required. (The thinking comes later when we try to figure out how to deal with a situation our reactions have made much worse.)

When James and John asked Jesus if he wanted them to call down fire on a Samaritan village that had refused him hospitality, it was a simple knee-jerk reaction. (I always wondered if this was in

---

29 Neale Donald Walsch, *When Everything Changes Change Everything* (Ashland, OR: EmNin Books, 2009), 84-85.

their power to accomplish). Jesus' response was a thoughtful, "*Let's just go on to another village*" (Luke 9:51f.).

The nickname "Sons of Thunder" already told us much about James and John. They had no idea that Jesus' ministry was eventually going to include these despised Samaritans. You wonder why their listening to Jesus' teaching had not brought them any further along. It is evident they had a long way to go. Question: Can I see myself in James and John? You know the answer to that!

QUESTIONS FOR REFLECTION AND DISCUSSION

1. What disturbed you most in this chapter and why do you think this was so?
2. Do you think that most of us have any idea of just how much more truth the Spirit of Jesus has for us?
3. Why do you think most of us are so uncomfortable with diversity, conflict, ambiguity, conflict, and paradox?

Nothing is more incredible than the incarnation.

John 1:14: *The Word became flesh and made his dwelling among us.*

The most incredible story in the history of religion is simply stated in these few words from the Gospel of John. It marks the beginning of the Christian calendar. It marks the beginning of God's most strategic move in his plan of salvation, redemption, and reconciliation with his creation. It is a miracle story at the highest level. It is not the miracle of our becoming like God but of God becoming a human being, becoming one of us. When I am asked if I believe the miracle stories in the Bible, my response is, "Well, once you accept the miracle of the Incarnation, all the others are a piece of cake." This is *the* miracle in the New Testament.

The earliest heresy the church confronted was the belief that Jesus did not become a real human being — he only appeared to be one. The earliest of the Gospels, Mark, goes out of its way to picture Jesus as fully human. The big debate during Jesus' lifetime was not about his humanity, it was about his divinity. The final "solution" offered by church councils was that Jesus was fully human and fully divine. No one has yet explained just how this works. Ink and blood have both been spilt in attempts to defend this faith assertion but it remains just that — our faith assertion.

There is another reality beyond this one.

When we talk about faith, we are not denying reality, we are shifting gears into another reality beyond this one. Science does this all the time with its discoveries both large and small that make us aware of realms we never before knew existed. The world of the biblical writers was exceedingly small but was large enough to include testimonies about another dimension that lies beyond this one. We continually encounter the phrase "by faith we believe" in the passages of the Bible. This does not mean they believed the absurd and ridiculous. It means they came to a faith-stance on the basis of what they heard and saw in Jesus of Nazareth as God's clearest and highest manifestation of himself in the world.

Jesus' humanity was not a bad thing. The book of Hebrews holds it is just because of that humanity that Jesus is now able to be our high priest (our advocate, our intercessor) who fully understands us because he fully became one of us. He understands us because he walked in our shoes for over thirty years and experienced everything we experience. This is a tough one for many to accept but it is a clear teaching of Scripture without which we have only a partial understanding of the Incarnation.

It still remains difficult to fully understand and explain.

From the book of Hebrews (NNT):

> We have then, in Jesus, the Son of God, a great high priest who has passed into the highest heaven; let us, therefore, hold fast to the faith which we have professed. Our high priest is not one unable to sympathize with our weaknesses, but one who has in every way been tempted exactly as we have, but without sin. Therefore, let us boldly draw near to the throne of love, to find pity and love for the hour of need. (4:14-16).
>
> Son though he was, he learned obedience from his sufferings, and being made perfect, he became to all those who obey him the source of eternal salvation. (4:8-9).

> *Now on this subject I have much to say, but it is difficult
> to explain it to you, because you have shown yourselves so slow to
> learn.* (4:11).

The only way we understand others is to take our place as a fully human person in a world of other fully human persons. We are united by our common humanity. This ought to generate compassion, mercy, forgiveness, and understanding among people but this is still one of the major tasks to be achieved in our world. The beginning of all positive relationships is to acknowledge that everyone we meet is a person created in the image of God, regardless of how distorted or marred that image may be. The "benediction" of a comedy TV show of some years ago sums it up: "Remember, we're all in this thing together."

MUSINGS FROM HITHER AND YON

God in Sandals.

Rachel Evans in *Faith Unraveled* has the above title for her chapter dealing with the Incarnation. The problem is those sandals take Jesus places many think he should not go and walk with people who are "the wrong kind." "To the Pharisees, Jesus just didn't fit the mold. His theology was too edgy, his friends too salacious, and his love too inclusive."[30]

> "The Son of Man came eating and drinking," says Jesus, "and they say, 'Look, a glutton and a drunkard.'" In other words, the Gospels record criticism of Jesus for being too high-spirited and joyful *in his own lifetime.* "Jesus and his disciples," says Father Clifford, "are criticized for living it up."[31]

I'll never forget a Bible study in my first church out of seminary. Our passage was the episode where Jesus turns water into

30 Rachel Evans, *Faith Unraveled*, 154.
31 James Martin, *Between Heaven and Mirth* (New York: HarperOne, 2011), 53.

wine at a wedding after the host's supply has become exhausted. Someone in the back of the room spoke up and said, "Well, we know it was Welchade; it wasn't alcoholic." Before I could think of an appropriate response, another person offered, "No, those people would have known the difference between good wine and Welchade. Plus, it was said to be the best wine that had been served. I do believe Jesus turned water into real wine but I have to confess: it has been an embarrassment to me all my life."

I didn't pursue the subject further but the embarrassment would have been even greater if those present for the study had been told that, according to the text, Jesus made between 120 and 180 gallons of wine. There are many lessons to be gained from Jesus first recorded "sign" in John's Gospel other than the quality and quantity of wine. God's provisions are abundant even to overflowing. In the two episodes of the feeding of the 5,000 and later the 4,000, the disciples are struck by not only how many people are fed with such few provisions, but the abundance of food that is left over after all have eaten their fill. Signs and miracles are acted parables and are always richer in meaning than a literal reading reveals.

Does Jesus reveal what God is really like?

One of my Calvinist critics said at a conference: "You cannot use Jesus to establish what God is like because Jesus is also human." I almost fell off my chair.

What then are we to make of statements such as "He who has seen me has seen the Father" (John 14:9); "Jesus discloses to us the very nature of God" (Heb. 1:3); and "in (Jesus) the fullness of the deity dwelled in bodily form" (Col. 2:9)? You say that "the incarnation is the clearest instance of God's accomodation to us." I prefer to say that the incarnation is the clearest instance of God's self-disclosure to us. The things that Jesus said and did are what God is like.[32]

---

32 Christopher A. Hall and John Sanders, *Does God Have a Future?*, 67.

The basis on which I interpret Scripture is by beginning with what I believe to be the highest and clearest revelation of all: Jesus Christ.

> *In the past God spoke to our ancestors through the prophets at many times and in various ways, but in these last days he has spoken to us by his Son... The Son is the radiance of God's glory and the exact representation of his being...* (Hebrews 1:1-3).

An important sidebar: There are numerous indications in both the Hebrew and Christian Scriptures that God is affected by what we do. As early as the Book of Genesis we have this observation before the flood episode: *The Lord regretted that he had made human beings on the earth, and his heart was deeply troubled.* The Incarnation has many examples of Jesus' feeling with us: Luke 7:13 reveals Jesus' response when he sees a widow's son being carried out of the city of Nain for burial: *The Lord was heart-sorry for her when he saw her* (BARCLAY).

The above reference is from the William Barclay translation which I highly recommend for its many inclusions of verb tenses and literal Greek translations. This often gives a much clearer meaning to a text like Matthew 7:7: *Keep on asking, and you will get; keep on seeking and you will find; keep on knocking, and the door will be opened for you.* This underscores Jesus' emphasis on persistence in prayer which can easily be missed in most translations.

Beginning with the highest revelation does not solve all exegetical problems but it does begin with what we understand to be the best picture of God's words and actions that we have in Scripture. The reason John Sander's critic (in the quote that begins this section) had a problem with Jesus humanity is that it pictures a God who feels with us, who is moved by our pain, and who, ultimately, suffers with us. I confess that this is deep theology but it is even at the heart of the Hebrew Scriptures in describing God's response to Hezekiah's prayer: *Thus says the Lord, the God of your ancestor David: I have heard your prayer, I have seen your tears; indeed, I will heal you; on the third day you shall go up to the house of the Lord. I will add fifteen years to your life* (2 Kings 20:5-6).

This announcement comes after Isaiah is commanded by God to tell the king to get his house in order because he is going to die. Things change because Hezekiah prays. God has a new plan for the king. When I announced in a sermon where I was guest minister that "God changed his mind about what he was going to do," the following week a seminary student who heard the sermon demanded that I no longer be allowed to preach in that church. He never told me why I was wrong in my interpretation of the text. I see in the life and ministry of Jesus many situations where things change because of Jesus' response to prayers and cries for mercy. If things can't change, why are we commanded to pray?

> *Is anyone among you sick? Let them call the elders of the church to pray over them and anoint them with oil in the name of the Lord and the prayer offered in faith will make them well; the Lord will raise them up* (James 5:14).

How can we understand others unless we share a common humanity?

> There's usually more than one person who can't handle your grieving, who offers no support at all.[33]
>
> But my favorite thoughtless statement — and I am not making this up — is this one: "I know just how you feel," one woman said. "My dog died two weeks ago."[34]

This woman simply hasn't lived long enough and experienced the kinds of losses of loved ones that bring us to the depths of grief and despair. I am not making light of the loss of a pet but, basically, no one should ever say, "I know just how you feel." We don't know how others are processing their grief. Grief has its own personal and

---

33   Candy Lightner & Nancy Hathaway, *Giving Sorrow Words* (New York: Warner Books, 1990), 40.
34   Ibid, 42.

unique signature for each of us. Our common experiences of loss, grief, and suffering should make us compassionate and create an empathy that enables us to stand with others in such times. Words are far less important than our simple presence.

> The British journalist Malcolm Muggeridge put it bluntly, maybe a little too bluntly: "I can say with complete truthfulness that everything I have learned in my 75 years in this world, everything that has truly enhanced and enlightened my existence, has been through affliction and not through happiness, whether pursued or attained."[35]

When Muggeridge speaks of those things that have "enhanced and enlightened" his existence, I understand what he is talking about. We don't like to hear about the world being a vale of soul-making but confessions of it being so are everywhere. Here is the testimony of Michael J. Fox:

> Because Parkinson's demanded of me that I be a better man, a better husband, father, and citizen, I often refer to it as a gift…I add this qualifier — it's the gift that keeps on taking — but it is a gift.[36]

Another surprising benefit of our humanity.

> There's a lovely Hasidic story of a rabbi who always told his people that if they studied the Torah, it would put Scripture on their hearts. One of them asked, "Why on our hearts, and not *in* them?" The rabbi answered, "Only God can put Scripture inside. But reading sacred text can put it on your hearts, and then when your hearts break, the holy words will fall inside."[37]

---

35 David Brooks, *The Second Mountain: The Quest for a Moral Life* (New York: Random House, 2019), 49.

36 Michael J. Fox, *Always Looking Up: The Adventures of an Incurable Optimist* (New York: Hyperion, 2009), 87.

37 Ann Lamott, *Plan B: Further Thoughts on Faith* (New York: Riverhead Books, 2005), 73.

One of the reasons I never complete my reading of any portion of Scripture is that on re-reading I always find something I never knew was there. Such a discovery is made because I am at a new place in life and some of my experiences have created an openness to new truth and understanding that has not been previously present. Anne Lamott was deeply moved by the response of a nurse from the Alzheimer's Association who was summoned because the family was unable to reach a decision on what was best to do for their mother. They confessed, "We don't know what we're doing. We don't know if we should put her in a home, and if so, when. We don't know what's true anymore." The nurse asked gently, "How *could* you know?"[38]

Such compassion and understanding cannot come from a book, only from living with families and patients who are experiencing the devastating effects of Alzheimer's. Standing with people, sharing their frustrations, dilemmas, and fears brings new perspectives to the wilderness journey these people are experiencing. How *could* they know? After all, they are only human.

QUESTIONS FOR REFLECTION AND DISCUSSION

1. Are you surprised to learn that the first heresy the church fought was the belief by some that Jesus was not fully human?
2. How do you think your humanity has helped you to be a more compassionate person?
3. How do you interpret 2 King's 20 and the reversal of a previously made decision on God's part?

---

38 Ibid, 139.

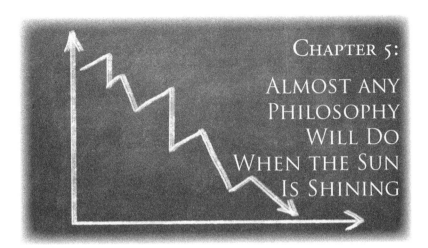

Chapter 5:
Almost Any Philosophy Will Do When the Sun Is Shining

A hole in the roof is fine during fair weather.

The song may advise to "Let a smile be your umbrella on a rainy, rainy day," but that is assuming those showers do not come with a weather alert. Even a large golf umbrella will provide no protection from damaging winds or a tornado. Almost any kind of protection will suffice during a gentle summer rain. A smile and a positive attitude are great assets to possess but when the destructive forces of life come at you with gale-force winds, you'd better have a different strategy.

Most self-help books provide some sort of practical wisdom which is not too bad to put in your philosophy kit. But the sun will not always be shining, the showers will not always be light, the winds will not always be calm, and the road will not always be well-paved. Sometimes we will find ourselves journeying through a valley as dark as death itself. When all the lights go out, when life seems to take everything from you, when all hope is gone, when your back is literally to the wall — what will be the philosophy that will sustain you?

What do you do when you're "up against it"?

At one time or another (and probably more than once) life deals us what appears to be a losing hand. The old "play the cards you are dealt" is not what we want to hear. Since we can't call for a re-deal (oh, how often I have wished for that possibility!), our only hope is for a game changer. Our only hope is for a wild card. Our only hope is for something beyond our power and ability.

Biblically speaking:

> *God is our refuge and strength, a very present help in trouble. Therefore, we will not fear, though the earth should change, though the mountains shake in the heart of the sea; though the waters roar and foam, though the mountains tremble with its tumult* (Psalm 46:1-3).

With the world falling apart in a seeming return to the original chaos before creation, the psalmist is confident of the help God will provide. The remainder of the psalm assures the reader that God will have the last word and will ultimately bring a cessation to the destructive forces. Verse 10 gives the stance one is to take in the midst of the turmoil: *Be still, and know that I am God.* Verse 7 is repeated as the conclusion to the psalm: *The Lord of hosts is with us; the God of Jacob is our refuge.*

The sustaining philosophy of this psalm is God's commitment to us and his purposes in the midst of a world seemingly out of control. Most of us have been blessed by the comfort, strength, and encouragement we have experienced from the presence of others who have stood with us in our personal storms of life. In periods of soul distress, we are to rest in the assurance that the God of Abraham, Isaac, and Jacob, the God of our Lord and Savior Jesus Christ, is with us. Many bear testimony to the gift of *shalom* (peace, a sense of security and well-being) that frequently becomes a greater reality in times of severe difficulty and stress.

There is no rescue team sent for us when our way is dark.

The sustaining philosophy provided in Scripture is not that when we are in the valley as dark as death itself (Psalm 23) God will turn on all the lights, but that he will be with us all the way through that darkness. This is the assurance that God is with us, that we are his, and that nothing can ever separate us from his love (Romans 8:38-39). When all is said and done, the only source of that kind of security is within us. This is the inner security which is the only kind of real security there is.

This is the philosophy that sustains us whether or not the sun is shining.

MUSINGS FROM HITHER AND YON.

It can happen.

My friend Greg grew up without rock-and-roll. "Movies and dancing were out too," he explained, "as was theology." Raised in a strict, King-James-only-church that closely followed the teachings of (name intentionally omitted), Greg describes his initial experience with Christianity as one that was "moralistic, reactionary, anti-intellectual, and atheological." "It was like drowning in a pool of shallow water," he said.[39]

Many of us did not discover just how shallow that pool of water was until a major crisis hit. My early church experience was the same as Greg's and I know what he is talking about. I never realized how thin the theology was until life demanded some things my faith could not supply.

I never want to knock the props out from under anyone who is being sustained by something that is simply not adequate for me. Usually, the less than adequate philosophy works because the larger questions are ignored and insights into just how much more there is are not allowed due to repeated warnings about reading

---

39 Rachel Evans, *Faith Unraveled,* 64.

and listening to "harmful and faith-destroying material". The guest speakers at my church, the recommended reading material, and the warnings that were issued kept my faith restricted and maintained the shallowness of which I was yet unaware.

There were many good people in my boyhood church and it was not until a scandal broke about the pastor's involvement with a high school senior that I discovered some of the anger and frustration that had been kept under lock and key. I don't remember a sermon that ever challenged me to go beyond the basics of "the fundamentals of the faith." Many of these "fundamentals" (much enlarged) are still a part of my faith, except for those like the charts from Revelation that predicted Christ's eminent return by giving names and dates that were simply not true to the biblical texts. I heard a lot about sin and judgment and very little about grace; very little about the calling that belongs to each of us in this world; very little about the opportunities and possibilities that can bring the joy to our lives Jesus said he had come to impart to each of us.

My biggest complaint was the anti-intellectual stance of our pastor who was always lashing out at some "liberal" person or, more frequently, some liberal university or seminary. The many questions I had about life and the narrowness of the faith being proclaimed were not being addressed. I really felt as though we had to check our minds at the door when we entered the sanctuary on Sunday. A repeated cry from the pulpit was, "Don't let college rob your young people of their faith!" My college and seminary experiences didn't subtract anything from my faith but gave me something that was richer and far more satisfying than the pool of shallow water in which I had been drowning.

Four of life's biggest questions.

Matthew Kelly is a Catholic writer who has much to say to all of us. I especially enjoyed his *Perfectly Yourself* in which he gives detailed suggestions on how to achieve God's goal for us in becoming the best version of ourselves. This is quantum leaps above a self-help book in which the emphasis is on personal fulfillment. This book is about fulfilling the purpose God has for each of us in our uniqueness.[40]

One of his more recent books contains what Kelly terms four of life's biggest questions. I believe they are the questions that any sustaining faith or philosophy must be able to take on. The questions are:[41]

Who am I?
What am I here for?
What matters most?
What matters least?

Faith that is able to address these issues must have depth all the way across. It does not have room for any shallowness — even around the edges.

QUESTIONS FOR REFLECTION AND DISCUSSION

1. The Bible clearly teaches that the storms of life come to all. What kind of a faith does this call for?
2. What in your faith has been most helpful to you when all the lights have gone out (Psalm 23)?
3. What is your response to Matthew Kelly's four of life's biggest questions? How have you attempted to answer them?

---

40 Matthew Kelly, *Perfectly Yourself* (New York: Ballantine Books, 2006).
41 Matthew Kelly, *The Biggest Lie in the History of Christianity* (Kakadu, Australia: no publisher listed, 2018), 13.

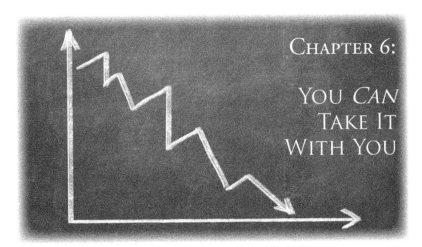

CHAPTER 6:

YOU *CAN*
TAKE IT
WITH YOU

Broadway does not have the last word.

Years ago, there was a Broadway play, later made into a movie, called *You Can't Take It With You.* The underlying thesis was that the accumulation of things might appear to be the goal of life but, in the end, everything is left behind — you can take nothing with you. It's not unlike the old quip, "I've never seen a Brinks' truck following a hearse." It parallels the question "How much did he leave?" with its expected answer, "He left it all." I Timothy 6:7 gives the full scope of that nothingness: *"For we brought nothing into this world, and we can take nothing out of it."*

If we are talking about material possessions, there is no doubt about the correctness of all these assertions. However, there appears to be another reality of eternal investments involved when Jesus commands:

> *Do not store up for yourselves treasures on earth, where moth and rust destroy, and where thieves break in and steal. But store up for yourselves treasures in heaven, where moth and rust do not destroy, and where thieves do not break in and steal. For where your treasure is, there your heart will be also.* (Matthew 6:19-22).

Which bank are you using?

This is not to be interpreted as chastisement for prudent management of resources, planning for retirement, or having an emergency fund in your budget. It speaks to the kind of life in Jesus' parable preceded by the warning: "*Watch out! Be on your guard against all kinds of greed: Life does not consist in an abundance of possessions."* The parable Jesus then tells is about a prosperous farmer who has such a bumper crop that his only solution is to build bigger barns. He will then be able to say to himself, "I have plenty of grain laid up for many years so I'll take life easy; eat, drink, and be merry." Jesus then gives the punch line: *But God said to him, "You fool! This night your life will be demanded from you. Then who will get what you have prepared for yourself?" This is how it will be with those who store up things for themselves but are not rich toward God.* (Luke 12:15-21).

Jesus is certainly going against the grain of modern culture when he maintains that life does not consist in the abundance of one's possessions or that one's worth as a human being depends on how much has been accumulated. Jesus' words are to be understood as judgment against those who live as though the only investments worth making are the ones in this life. Jesus shifts the focus to eternal investments that no fluctuating market can devalue. He implies there are things you can take with you when this earthly pilgrimage is ended.

You can make eternal investments.

Whenever I use Psalm 90 for a funeral homily, a major emphasis is on the final verse: *May the favor of the Lord our God rest on us; establish the work of our hands for us — yes, establish the work of our hands.* This conclusion seems necessary in a psalm that speaks about God's everlastingness (verse 2) and the brevity of our lives (verse 16). It is a plea for God to make our works endure beyond this brief span of years.

My take on this psalm (and many New Testament passages) is that in the context of our resurrection faith, we are making eternal investments. We are building relationships for eternity, we are growing in grace for eternity, we are learning the disciplines of the Spirit life for eternity. I firmly believe that when we leave this world, we take everything with us — we take all we have become, we take all we are. Any deeds of kindness, love, and compassion we perform are deeds done for eternity. In Matthew 10:42, Jesus promises that even a cup of cold water given in his name will be rewarded.

To *establish the work of our hands* tells us God is in the remembering business. In response to the questions: "A hundred years from now what difference will it make? Who will remember that we lived and what we have done?", the biblical answer is: God will. A hundred years from now, a thousand years from now, an eternity from now God will remember us and our deeds because we matter and what we do matters. The Scripture teaches that God will establish not only us but also what we have done. Meaning: he will maintain us and our eternal investments.

Psalm 90 opens with the proclamation of God's everlastingness which it then compares to our brief time of seventy or eighty years on earth (verse 16). A key verse for reflection is verse 12: *Teach us to number our days, that we may gain a heart of wisdom.* If we have unlimited time, postponing things we ought to do is not so bad. Scarlett comforts herself with her last spoken line in *Gone With the Wind:* "After all, tomorrow is another day." What we all know is that tomorrow may *not* be another day. We are to receive each day as a gift and use it to accomplish what should be done in that day.

Psalm 90 ends with a twice repeated prayer of the psalmist that gives our deeds an eternal sounding in a psalm that speaks about the brevity of existence: *Establish the work of our hands for us — yes, establish the work of our hands.* God will make certain that we don't "leave it all" when we leave this world. All that is really important, all that we really are, we will take with us.

MUSINGS FROM HITHER AND YON.

Not your ordinary piece of furniture

Thomas Merton: "The particular grace of a Shaker chair is due to the fact that it was made by someone capable of believing that an angel might come and sit on it."[42]

My wife and I have made multiple visits to Shaker Village, a short drive out of Lexington, Kentucky. Although the community no longer exists, its stories and its handiwork remain to be experienced in a setting that has preserved many of the original buildings. Merton has captured the spirit of Shaker craft in a single sentence. Shakers lived with the realization of just how thin the veil is that separates this world and "the other world." If you believe you are not simply making a chair but you are producing a work of spiritual significance, it shows in the quality of your work.

The second half of life

Angeles Arrien has written a book that views life as a whole and not as a good first half with youth, health, purpose, and hope and a second half with decline and oblivion. In another book, I wrote that it almost seems as though aging is the unpardonable sin. In a culture that is youth oriented there is not much indication of satisfaction that can come with advancing years. Enter Arrien with these words:

The second half of life presents us with the opportunity to develop increased depth, integrity, and character — or not.[43]

I love the "or not" at the end of the sentence because that is the big decision we all must make in our later years. With many things no longer possible, what will we do with the areas of life that

---

42 Robert Ellsberg, *The Saints' Guide to Happiness* (New York: North Point Press, 2003), 46.

43 Angeles Arrien, *The Second Half of Life* (Boulder: Sounds True, 2005), 5.

present us with the greatest opportunities? These are opportunities to develop those things that we will be taking with us when we leave this world: increased depth (wisdom), integrity, and character. Whenever I suggest that "we enter the next life on the level at which we leave this one", I always get a number of puzzled looks and a number of questions. Some have always believed that somehow "sainthood" will be slipped over us like a celestial robe, and we will go floating into a new dimension of existence that makes us comfortable with all the truly great saints of old.

Well, I think not. First, there is no biblical evidence for such a view. "To be with the Lord" is the basic promise of what happens when we leave here and there is very little detail in Scripture about the next life except that it will be "in the Father's house". As God has not forced anything on us now, it is just not reasonable to believe that suddenly he will zap us with all the qualities he wanted us to have in this life. No. I believe in his grace he will receive us as we are, and we will enter upon a new life of growth and development that begins exactly where we left off. What would make the next life more exciting than to believe that it is a place of continual becoming?

What is really left.

In his commentary on Jesus' parable of the rich man and Lazarus (Luke 16), Helmut Thielicke writes:

> What are you apart from your possessions, your functions, and your relations? What being remains, and will go with you, when you have to leave what you have? What is your ultimate identity? What are you as a person apart from these penultimate things and external attachments? What is left of you and your being when you are subjected to the subtraction of death? This is, as it were, the most pointed of all the questions death puts to us.[44]

---

44 Helmut Thielicke, *Living With Death* (Grand Rapids: William B. Eerdmans, 1983), 16.

I wish I had written that paragraph because it summarizes in clear, concise, and frightening language the one inevitable in life that no one can escape. I have read of workshops in which participants have been asked to write their obituaries. They are to tell how they want to be remembered, the things they want to accomplish and the way they want to leave this world. I believe another question for such an exercise would be: What kind of a person do you want to be when you leave this world? That is the work of a lifetime, and we should not wait until the second half of life to take up the task (although most of us do).

QUESTIONS FOR REFLECTION AND DISCUSSION

1. How do you interpret Jesus' command to store up for ourselves treasures in heaven?
2. How does Psalm 90 speak to you about gaining a heart of wisdom?
3. What kind of motivation do you believe you could bring to your daily work if you had the "Shaker chair" perspective?

I do so wish it were so!

I often wish my life were like a movie, where finally I could hear the director shout, "That's a wrap!" This would signify that a segment of my life, an episode, a significant piece of my life-story is finally as it should be. I have finally gotten something altogether.

This, however, is only for the movies. It doesn't work this way in real life. We keep trying to get it right. We keep trying to improve the way we relate to others. We keep trying to be more patient with family members who seem to come up with new ways to drive us crazy. We keep working on maintaining our calm in traffic when all the worst drivers seem to be on the road at the same time. We keep working on reducing our consumption of "breaking news" in order to lower our anger and frustration levels. We keep working on trying to be that better person, the person we know we were meant to be, instead of that flawed human being who keeps pushing his/her way to the forefront.

This is only a partial list of the many things I am trying to get together at the age of 84. My earlier life was marked by the frequent observation, "If only I could...." The assumption was that this *one* thing would make all the difference. Often, it did make a difference but it turned out to be only one of the many things it was going to take to get it all together. I did not realize the complexity of life and its demands. Increasing age brings the recognition of that increasing complexity I discover about myself as a human being. It's not unlike what scientists keep discovering about the complexity of our world.

It may not be so bad after all.

I have come to believe this may not be such a bad thing after all. It certainly is a lesson in humility and a major reason to be more compassionate and understanding with other human beings who appear to be having just as much difficulty getting it all together as I do. "Why can't they get their lives straightened out?" is the question we often address to those who have made a real mess of things. And then I reflect back on times when I have made a real mess of things. It reminds me of a book title, "*Bless This Mess and Other Prayers.*" The inability to achieve order and harmony in my life is simply another reminder that I had better get some outside help. This may involve much on the human level but it always involves help on the spiritual level. Adam and Eve were tempted to believe that eating the forbidden fruit would bring them to the place where they would finally be self-sufficient and could get along without God. That place is unattainable on the human level. I am reminded of that every day.

I once read a book titled "*Let's Hear It For Imperfection.*" This harkens back to Chapter 4 which I might have called "Let's Hear It For Our Humanity." I almost gave this chapter the caption, "Imperfection Is Here To Stay." When we demand perfection of ourselves, we are demanding the impossible. This is not to suggest that we should cease in the attempt to give our best to everything we do. This is not to suggest that we set such low standards for ourselves that we easily reach our goals. This is not to suggest that we become satisfied with low levels of performance in everything we do. It is simply the confession that given all we know to do with the very best intentions and efforts we can muster, there will always be things we didn't get quite right.

I continue to be a work in progress.

When I was graduated from seminary and became senior pastor of a church, I thought I was adequately prepared to do a masterful job. What I quickly became aware of was how much "on the job training" was going to be necessary to discharge the calling I was certain I had received. What I did not know was that the same awareness would be mine after more than sixty years of pastoral ministry. I never completed my on the job training! I continued to be aware of areas that needed more work (or someone would be kind enough to point them out to me). I never really got it all together in pastoral or church consultant ministry. But I did get better at what I was doing and this I finally realized was what life, and the life of faith, is all about.

I have somewhere (now safely tucked away in some unknown file) a prayer which I have always treasured. It goes something like this:

> O Lord, I'm know I'm not what I should be,
> I know I'm not what I could be,
> I know I'm not what you intend for me to be,
> And I know I'm not what I'm going to be.
> But I thank you, Lord,
> I know I'm not what I used to be.

What could be a better goal in life? I do believe God intends for us to grow daily in His grace and wisdom. Be the increments ever so small, each day is to find us more the person God has created us to be. This seems to me a far better goal than attempting to get it all together. In the Gospels, the people who believed they had it all together were the very people Jesus couldn't do anything for. They were beyond his help because they didn't think they needed any. My take: how can it possibly get any worse than this?

MUSINGS FROM HITHER AND YON

A Most Helpful Quote for Me.

> Spirituality is not about being fixed; it is about God's being present in the mess of our unfixedness...Look at the Bible. Its pages overflow with messy people.[45]

I confess that the book quoted above is one I bought because of the title, *Messy Spirituality*. I had tried perfect spirituality and missed that, so perhaps this was the book that described the kind of spirituality I could achieve. And it does. Beginning in the Book of Genesis, we have what I would describe as a messy family from the outset. We'll ignore the initial mess in the Garden and begin with the patron saint of the Bible. Abraham hardly gets underway in his God-directed journey, before, in a brief detour to Egypt, he passes off his wife as his sister (Genesis 12:10f).

We are not told Sarai's response to Abram's request (their names have not yet been changed), but his perception is that she is so beautiful the Egyptians will kill him in order to get her. The lie carries the day. Serious diseases are inflicted on Pharaoh and his household; someone ties the cause of this to Pharaoh having taken Sarai into the palace harem. Abram and his household are sent on their way while we are left with difficult exegesis: Pharaoh and his household suffer because of Abram's lie and there is no divine messenger sent to chastise (or punish) him for what he has done.

The remainder of Genesis follows this family in its many mis-happenings. Dysfunctional is the word we would use for them today but God's word for them is "Chosen." I find the account encouraging because it confirms what Yaconelli says in the above quote: "Spirituality is about God being with us in the mess of our unfixedness." I would add: and bringing about his plan and purpose as he works in and through that unfixedness. Imperfect

---

45 Michael Yaconelli, *Messy Spirituality* (Grand Rapids: Zondervan, 2002), 13.

people adorn the pages of Scripture. You will find no other kind. I'm glad the Psalms continually remind us of God's two greatest attributes: Love and Faithfulness. They are spoken of as eternal. They are spoken of as God's great grace-gifts to all of us — in spite of the fact that we don't have it all together.

The biggest discovery.

> Worldly means you think the solution to your inner problems is in the world outside. You think that if you change things outside, you'll be okay. But nobody has ever truly become okay by changing things outside. There's always the next problem. The only real solution is to take the seat of witness consciousness and completely change your frame of reference.[46]

Some will pass on Singer's book if they read the endorsement by Ray Kurzweil on the back cover: "East is East and West is West, but Michael Singer bridges these two great traditions in a radiant treatise on how to succeed in life from our spiritual quest to our everyday tribulations." The brief paragraph is a perfect illustration of what he has done and this valuable insight is one that is clearly taught in the New Testament: the key to a transformed life is not getting the world arranged as we would have it but dealing with our attitudes, perspectives, and keeping our frame of reference that of a Kingdom citizen (The Sermon on the Mount).

We certainly will never be able to get it all together if we major on trying to change our circumstances. Big sidebar: this is not to say that some things do not need to be changed. The Serenity Prayer of AA is known to most of us: "God, grant me the serenity to accept the things I cannot change, courage to change the things I can, and wisdom to know the difference." Most alcoholics readily confess that they blamed their addition on circumstances that made it almost impossible not to drink: a spouse who just didn't understand, a boss who made unreasonable demands, etc. The list was endless. Sobriety finally came when the confession was made,

---

46 Michael A. Singer, *The Unfettered Soul,* 16.

"The problem is me. Regardless of my circumstances I can choose to remain sober. Whatever happens does not cause me to take a drink. I drink because I choose to do so."

The above paragraph is much simplified but the meaning is clear. Once we continue to view our problems as "out there," there will never be an end to the reasons for failing to be the kind of person we ought to be. Through the years I have made the discovery we all make sooner or later: "there will always be something wrong that *causes* me to stay bent out of shape." Once I confess that the cause is not "out there" but in me, I have put the focus in the right place. And, of course, this new focus only means that all that has been previously said about our being works in progress now means we are concentrating our efforts in the right place.

A confession that reveals an all too common problem.

> After a sermon in which I spoke of my often unsuccessful struggles to live by the truths in the biblical text for the day, a choir member let me know that he did not want to hear of my difficulties with discipleship. This young man wanted a minister who "has it all together," a minister who can serve as a model and even be viewed on a pedestal....Another member said to me, "We don't expect you, our minister, to be like the rest of us."[47]

If you are unfamiliar with the church world, it is almost impossible to imagine members of a congregation addressing such comments to their pastor. What these members were asking was simply impossible...period. Welton Gaddy speaks openly about the hospitalization that resulted from his attempts to live up to such unreasonable demands. He is open about the many aspects of life changes that were a part of his recovery but one stands out to me:

> During an interview with a reporter covering a conference at which I was speaking, I was asked, "What do you

47   C. Welton Gaddy, *A Soul Under Siege* (Louisville: Westminster/John Knox Press, 1991), 37.

know now that you did not know, and maybe wish you had known, earlier in your ministry?" Typically, when dealing with a reporter, responses are formed slowly and deliberately. This time was different. Immediately I said, "I realize that I am a human being."[48]

Perhaps we need a little humor to lighten things up and provide a summary to all we've talked about.

Dan Bennett: "Probably nothing in the world arouses more false hopes that the first four hours of a diet."[49]

QUESTIONS FOR REFLECTION AND DISCUSSION

1. Do you accept the premise of this chapter's title?
2. What do you think about Yaconelli's thesis that spirituality is not about God's fixing us but about his being with us in the mess of our unfixedness?
3. Have you experienced a time when you finally gave up trying to change something "out there" and looked for a "solution" within yourself?

---

48 Ibid, 34.
49 M. *Scott* Peck, *An Anthology of Wisdom* (Kansas City: Ariel Books, 1996), 205.

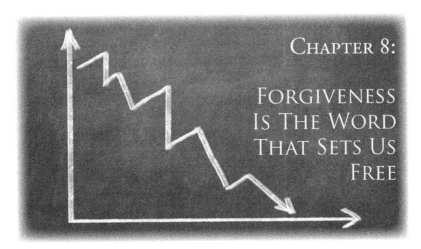

The gate to freedom does seem to be narrow.

When Peter asked his famous question about forgiveness, he coupled it with an answer that he must have felt was worthy of commendation from his Teacher.

> *Then Peter came to Jesus and asked, "Lord, how many times shall I forgive someone who sins against me? Up to seven times?" Jesus answered, "I tell you, not seven times, but seventy-seven times."* (Matthew 18:31-32).

The consensus among the rabbis of the day seems to have been that three was the number of times for required forgiveness. Peter assumed he was being generous when he added four more to that. Jesus' response struck a fatal blow to all such calculations when he replied that seven was totally inadequate. Either seventy-seven or seven times seventy (a footnote to verse 32 indicates the number given can be translated either way) puts forgiveness outside mathematical considerations. There is no counting in forgiveness.

The prayer many of us offer on a regular basis contains the phrase *forgive us our trespasses as we forgive those who trespass against us.* This indicates that forgiveness is a daily ongoing affair (both for us and those who need our forgiveness). A possible translation of that verse is an alarming one: *forgive us our transgressions in the same measure as we forgive those who transgress against us.* Another verse is even more disturbing: *If you do not forgive others their sins, your Father will not forgive your sins* (Matthew 6:15). I take the meaning to be that if we refuse to forgive others then we have closed the door through which God's forgiveness flows to us. It's a tough text regardless of how you interpret it.

We are the ones who need to be set free.

The lesson to be gained is how important our forgiveness of others is to our own spiritual lives. There is much emphasis in the Christian faith on our need to be forgiven in order to receive salvation and eternal life. Here is the other side of that coin showing the need to have a forgiving spirit in order to set ourselves free from judgment, vengeance, and even hatred — all of which keep us bound in a prison of our own making.

It is beyond the scope of this chapter to fully explore the many dimensions of forgiveness. A few things must be said. True forgiveness is neither quick or easy. Just as God's forgiveness came with the cost of a cross, so our forgiveness is costly. We must give up our role as judge and jury and be willing to see what part we played in the hurt we experienced. We must have the same kind of compassion for our offender that God continues to have for us in our offenses. We must be committed to a ministry of reconciliation to which Paul says we have all been called. We are to be in the business of bridge building and hands across the divide.

The time forgiveness needs to complete its work is usually not brief.

When the hurt is deep and the pain is ongoing, it takes time to do our grief work and get ready to begin the process of forgiveness. It is a process — it is not an instant transaction. In giving a recent lecture on C. S. Lewis, I mentioned his acknowledgment of just how difficult it was for him to forgive. As a teenager his father enrolled him in a boarding school with a headmaster who was brutal and sadistic in his treatment of his students. (He was later certified insane and committed to an institution). In Lewis' *Letters to An American Lady* he confesses that, after trying for years to forgive that headmaster, he realizes he has finally been able to do it. The date of his letter indicates this was a full fifty years after the pain and humiliation of that boarding school. The point is that forgiveness was in the making all that time.

Through the years I have officiated at some weddings in which my instructions were to take great care in the seating of the families. Usually these were families fractured by divorce (some multiple) with various sets of spouses and children. Some were not on speaking terms and the bride wanted peace, at least for the wedding. This brings to mind the many family members who choose not to speak to one another because of some past slight or misunderstanding (frequently involving money and estates). The divides that have been created can only be crossed by forgiveness which each side is waiting for the other to offer first.

The Power of Forgiveness.

Forgiveness is the power that brings together people, communities, and nations. We often forget it is a power that belongs to each of us. When God looked at his world with all its sin (missing the mark and falling short of the glory God intends in our lives), he came up with only one solution: forgiveness. That still remains the solution for our tangled relationships and our combative communities. It is the power to set other people free for a new beginning. And lest we forget, it is the power to set us free for a new beginning. Our forgiveness of others is so important that Jesus still stuns us with his demand for our giving up measuring it out. It is to keep rolling out just as God's forgiveness keeps on rolling out to us through Jesus Christ our Lord.

MUSINGS FROM HITHER AND YON

Why it should be done.

Ultimately, forgiveness is usually about one thing — "This is for me, not for you." Hatred is exhausting; forgiveness, or even just indifference, is freeing. To quote Booker T. Washington, "I shall allow no man to belittle my soul by making me hate him."[50]

There was a time when I would have disagreed with Sapolsky but I have come to believe he is on target with the basic reason we need to forgive. Refusing to forgive eats away at us; it feeds negativity and resentment. It does nothing to "punish" the person we refuse to forgive; it is an ongoing punishment of ourselves. We need to be set free from the negative emotions that sap away at our energy for living. We need to forgive so that we can be set free to become the persons we are meant to become.

The goal is to become a forgiving person.

Jesus' conversation with Peter about the number of times one should forgive settles forever the mathematics of forgiveness — keeping score is out. Paula Huston insists that the goal is to become a forgiving person.[51] Jesus was a forgiving person. God is a forgiving God. I continue to be amazed that whenever we ask to be forgiven and open our lives to receive it, the healing of God's redeeming love always flows in. Jesus was accused of being soft on sin because of his association with many whom the religious leaders of his day labeled "sinners." He appeared soft on sin because he was in the forgiveness and transformation business. He was in the business of bringing people to God and to one another. There was no picking and choosing of who (or what) would be forgiven.

50   Robert M. Sapolsky, *Behave*, 642.
51   Paula Huston, *Forgiveness: following Jesus into radical forgiveness* (Brewster: Paraclete Press, 2008), 103.

Growing up, I head many sermons on "The Unpardonable Sin." I have concluded from the biblical evidence that the unpardonable sin is the one for which someone does not want to be forgiven. Jesus certainly never met anyone to whom he said, "Sorry. Your sins fall outside the category of my forgiveness." No person, no sin, was beyond his forgiveness. It is obvious that is the model for us. Some appear to have a built-in detection system that lets them know which sins are worse than others. (Note: the worse ones are always those of others!) Jesus' command in Matthew 7:1, "*Do not judge,*" with the illustration of the speck and log, pictures just how difficult it is to know which are the "awful" sins and which are the "not so awful." The teaching of Scripture is that all sin is "awful" because it means we are missing the mark and falling short of the glory God intends in our lives.

Whose job is this anyway?

Being a forgiving person keeps us in the position of being able to fulfill the role to which God has called all of us: *the ministry of reconciliation* (2 Corinthians 5:18). Surveys repeatedly reveal that the average non-churchgoer is convinced "judgmental" characterizes most congregations. Biblically, the final judgment belongs to God (Romans 14:12 — *We will all give an account of ourselves to God),* but I also believe that includes all the judgments along the way. What would be the effect on us and those around us if we simply gave up the habit of judging and decided that really was God's prerogative after all?

Perhaps one of the reasons we have such a difficult time leaving this assignment to God is that we have a tough time accepting and feeling forgiven. Too many of us struggle with guilt due to sins we have already confessed and attempted to undo as much of the damage as possible. (Note: "undoing as much of the damage as possible" is not a requirement for forgiveness but is the result of one of the changes brought about by the power of forgiveness dominating our behavior.) When we feel forgiven, know that it came to us as

God's free gift, and realize how little we deserved it, the stage is set for living far less judgmentally and far more compassionately.

QUESTIONS FOR REFLECTION AND DISCUSSION

1. How do you interpret Matthew 6:15 (if we don't forgive others God won't forgive us)?
2. What do you think it means to be involved in the ministry of reconciliation?
3. Do you believe it is fair to level the charge of "judgmental" against the average church today?

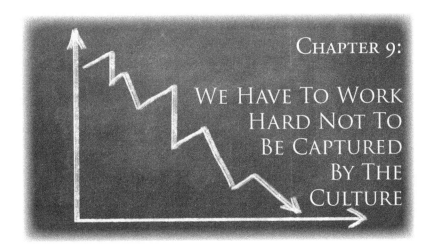

CHAPTER 9:

WE HAVE TO WORK
HARD NOT TO
BE CAPTURED
BY THE
CULTURE

The culture is a powerful force.

It appears we have had difficulty taking seriously Paul's admonition in Romans 12:2: *Do not conform to the patterns of this world, but be transformed by the renewing of your mind.* In plain English: do not think like the world thinks but think with your new mind as a follower of the Way. Don't let the standards the world establishes determine the way you will live your life. Don't allow the popular criteria for success become the benchmarks for determining how well you are doing. Allow the new perspectives of Kingdom citizenship (as clearly outlined in the Sermon on the Mount) be the way you see things. Let this new reality be the reality that determines your priorities.

Whenever the Bible speaks of the "world" in a negative sense, it is talking about life lived apart from the will and purpose of God. It is talking about living life as though there were no higher standards or demands than those we set for ourselves. It is all about looking out for number one. It is all about a life of competition in which we see ourselves part of a dog-eat-dog world. It is all about getting ahead regardless of the cost to others. It is all about adopting the standards the culture has drawn up for us.

In the case of ministers, a simple illustration will suffice. In most meetings involving a group of pastors, when anyone asks,

"How is your church doing these days?" the response usually comes with numbers — both of persons in the pews and the size of collections. Our success is determined by the increase in both of these. The larger the church, the more successful you are. The greater the numbers, the more "God is blessing you." It is impossible to find such criteria for success in the Bible.

The biblical formula for success.

Biblical speaking, the one criterion that is always mentioned for "success" is faithfulness. In Jesus' famous parable of the talents (it is really about bags of gold as Today's New International Version makes clear), the master of the house gives three servants different quantities of gold to invest: five bags, two bags, and one bag. When he returns for the accounting, the first two have doubled what they were given. To each, the same commendation is given: "*Well done, good and faithful servant! You have been faithful....* The third servant simply buried what he had received and returns it intact. He is told, "*You wicked lazy servant....*" He has done nothing with what he has been entrusted. He is not faithful as a servant. The criterion for success has nothing to do with how much each servant is given but on their faithfulness with what has been received (Matthew 25:14-30).

The measure of judgment for success is whether or not we have been faithful with what we have been given and the calling that belongs to us. It has nothing to do with the size of our giftedness or how big a splash we make in the media. It has nothing to do with the amount of recognition we receive. It has nothing to do with the level of applause we can elicit. It has everything to do with our being faithful to the task that belongs to us. It is impossible not to quote Mother Teresa's well-known philosophy: "We are not called to do great things; we are called to do small things with great love."

Everybody can be a winner...if....

We often hear, "In life's great game there are winners and losers." The culture gives itself high marks for pointing out those who are winners. In God's great game of life, everybody can be a winner. All you have to do is to exercise faithfulness in the calling that belongs to you — regardless of what that calling is or of how insignificant it seems. My philosophy: no calling is insignificant. Brother Lawrence is "famous" for "washing pots and pans for the glory of God." Doing KP in a monastery for all of his life, he was later recognized as a saint. His writings became a classic devotional book. He became all he was meant to become because he faithfully fulfilled the task to which he was certain he had been called.

The reward of the ages will be for us to hear the words, "Well done, good and faithful servant." This is something the world can never offer.

MUSINGS FOR HITHER AND YON

Spiritual Sanity

Spiritual sanity requires us to question the voices that are guiding our lives. It asks us to determine what inner and world values are leading us to believe, think, feel, and act the way we do. If we are to do this, we must have a critical eye for what is around us.[52]

In order to achieve this kind of spiritual sanity there must be some pretty substantial chunks of time devoted to meditation and reflection. The Gospels give some clear indicators of how much Jesus withdrew from the world in order to keep his Kingdom perspective intact. Even his disciples had other plans for the way messiahship should work: it had to do with power, authority, rule, and order. There was nothing in their plan that called for sacrifice.

---

52   Robert Wicks, *After 50* (New York: Paulist Press, 1997), 19.

In the above quote, Wicks calls for keeping a "critical eye" on what is around us. Many writers contend that critical thinking is one of the most important things we can teach our young people to do. They also bemoan the fact that it seems to be in very short supply among the adult population. My Dad's favorite response to a request for a decision on some difficult issue was: "I'll need time to mull that over." Whatever you call it, set aside time for determining what values are leading you to believe, think, feel, and act the way you do.

A bit of monastic wisdom

> Monastic wisdom flies in the face of many popular notions about both the kind of work we do and how we perform it. As Benedict decreed, a pot in the kitchen was to be no less venerated than a chalice on the altar. For Benedict, all types of work held the potential of offering intimacy with God, as well as personal happiness — and therefore obliging our best effort.[53]

Popular culture is guilty of assigning value both to what a person does and the person who does it. The Rule of Benedict ought to be the rule for all work: "a pot in the kitchen is to be no less venerated than a chalice on the altar". If the calling is yours, if the work is yours, it is indeed what should be termed "holy orders". The dedication Brother Lawrence brought to the washing of pots and pans was revealed only after his writings disclosed his commitment to doing it for the glory of God.

One of the self-help classics cited by Tom Butler-Bowdon in *50 Self-Help Classics* is *In Search of Character and Calling* by James Hillman who writes: "One's calling becomes a calling to honesty rather than to success, to caring and loving rather than to achieving. In this definition, life itself is the great work."[54] This brings calling to the level where it belongs: it has to do with our not only

---

53   Paul Wilkes, *Beyond the Walls* (New York: Image Books, 1999), 186.
54   *Robert Butler-Bowdon, 50 Self-Help Classics, 170.*

performing a task which we believe is uniquely ours, but in the process becoming the person we are meant to become.

What do you do?

Will Campbell frequently seemed to come at life and faith from a stance that caught us off guard. Here is an illustration of one I just came across:

> Usually when I am introduced to someone, he or she will ask, "And what do you do, Mr. Campbell?" If I am in a frivolous mode, I sometimes respond, "What do I do about what?"
>
> If I am more charitable, I might say, "I write rare books. At least, my royalty statements indicate that they are rare."
>
> Jesus never asked people what they did for money. His concern was, "How do you justify yourself?" The ultimate inference was, "At the end of your life, what have you done to leave the world a little better place than the one you entered?"[55]

Like a good parable, no comment of mine can possibly add anything.

Questions for Reflection and Discussion

1. Where do you believe you picked up your ideas about what it means to be a success in life?
2. What do you think about Robert Wicks' prescription for spiritual sanity?
3. Do you agree that Jesus' teaching about success in the parable discussed above has to do with faithfulness with whatever has been entrusted to us?

---

55 Will Campbell, *Soul Among Lions* (Louisville: John Knox Press, 1999), 35-36.

CHAPTER 10:

UNBELIEF, DOUBT AND DISCOURAGEMENT CONTINUE TO BE A PART OF FAITH

A strange text about the effectiveness of imperfect faith.

Mark 9:24 is a perfect example of the kind of faith most of us have but are hesitant to make the confession the father in the text was quick to make. As the father of an epileptic son, he implored Jesus, *"If you can do anything, take pity on us and help us."* (9:22) Jesus reversed the question and responds, *"If you can? Everything is possible for the one who believes."* Immediately the boy's father exclaimed, *"I do believe; help me overcome my unbelief!"*

The episode ends with Jesus healing the son. Evidently, a less than perfect faith on the part of the father was sufficient. I don't know that I have ever had any other kind of faith. Perhaps there is no other kind available for those of us who are saddled with humanity. "All you need is more faith" has been spoken by more than one person to an individual struggling with some serious issue. I see the point of the text as the call to exercise the faith we have in any situation, recognizing that it will always be mixed with some measure of unbelief. I believe that is the best most of us mortals can do.

Doubt and discouragement are woven into the gospel stories.

A text that appears to have frequently gone unnoticed is Matthew 28:16-17: *Then the eleven disciples went to Galilee, to the mountain where Jesus had told them to go. When they saw him, they worshiped him; but some doubted.* And we thought the resurrection appearances were sure things! If we had seen him on the other side of the cross, wouldn't that have been enough? Wouldn't the testimony of so many witnesses that "He is alive!" have been all that was needed? Evidently not for everyone, because Matthew records: *but some doubted.* Is he talking about some of the eleven disciples? These are the only ones he mentions as being with Jesus on the mountain. It seems that Thomas was not the only one who had a tough time with the idea of someone (even Jesus) coming back from the dead. We wish Matthew had unpacked just what kind of doubt they had and the reasons for their doubting. It reminds me so much of the response the late Carlyle Marney made when asked if he believed in resurrection: "Most of the time". I leave you to wrestle with that on your own.

Another text I want to add to this mix comes from Paul: *We do not want you to be uninformed, brothers and sisters, about the troubles we experienced in the province of Asia. We were under great pressure, far beyond our ability to endure, so that we despaired of life itself"* (2 Corinthians 1:8). This sounds like the depths of discouragement to me and from someone who constantly told us to rejoice and be positive about the life of faith. If you read carefully, Paul's humanity and frailty have a way of bringing him down a notch to two from the perfect sainthood to which so many have elevated him.

These three words — unbelief, doubt, and discouragement — show up on the pages of Scripture to remind us that they will inevitably show up in our lives. For those who seek "a perfect faith," I only say, "Lots of luck!" For most of us the best we can do is to ask for strength and courage to decrease the amount of unbelief, doubt, and discouragement that appear to be a part of the life of even the greatest of saints. I immediately think of Elijah, who, following God's great fireworks show on Mount Carmel, took flight from the wrath of Queen Jezebel and wound up in a cave of fear and self-pity (See I Kings 18f.). Even what we perceive to be the great miracles of Scripture don't seem to have the faith-producing effects we would have expected. After God's parting of the waters to permit the people to escape from Pharaoh's army, hardly any time passes before they are ready to stone Moses and go back to Egypt. What kind of miracle does it take to produce an unshakable faith? That's your question. I have no answer for it. (The only one that comes close for me is the one cited by Frederick Buechner in the Musings section which follows.)

I don't believe making progress in faith has anything to do with seeking to reach the goal of perfection. It has everything to do with growing incrementally in all the dimensions of life. Quantum leaps are rare (and usually short-lived). For most of us our daily prayer remains that of the desperate father, *"I do believe. Help me overcome by unbelief."*

MUSINGS FROM HITHER AND YON

Can God provide anything that will remove all doubt?

Frederick Buechner: "Not the least of my problems is that I can hardly even imagine what kind of an experience a genuine, self-authenticating religious experience would be. Without somehow destroying me in the process, how could God reveal himself in a way that would leave no room for doubt? If there were no room for doubt, there would be no room for me."[56]

To my mind, Buechner has presented the most succinct argument for God leaving room for doubt in our faith experience. The Hebrew Scriptures are full of stories of people who experienced

---

56 Frederick Buechner, *Listening to Your Life* (New York: HarperSanFrancisco, 1992), 91.

some of the most spectacular of God's miracles and only a few verses later are full of doubt and fear. This is a good time to remember that, biblically speaking, the opposite of faith is not doubt but fear. Numerous times Jesus asks his disciples, "Why are you afraid? Where is your faith?" Adverse circumstances always seem to be shaking up the faith of even those closest to Jesus.

A confession many did not want to hear.

The revelations in Mother Teresa's letters and journals, collected by Brain Kolodiejchuk, M.C., in *Mother Teresa: Come Be My Light,* talked about her painful "dark night" — a long period of prayer when it felt as though God were absent — and reminded people that silence is common, even in the lives of the saints. Many believers were astonished, even scandalized, that she spoke frequently of not feeling God's presence in her prayer. Some secular critics even pointed to her descriptions of silence as proof that her faith was weak. Or that God did not exist.

But silence is a part of any relationship.[57]

I found her confession refreshing because it only affirmed her humanity. It only affirmed that real faith contains real struggle and real periods of "the dark night of the soul." This does not mean faith is not real. This does not mean that God is not real.

The necessary tension.

You cannot bypass the necessary tension of holding contraries and inconsistencies together, if you are to live on this earth.[58]

---

57   James Martin, *The Jesuit Guide to Almost Everything* (New York: HarperOne, 2010), 139.
58   Richard Rohr, *The Naked Now*, 106.

I guess we're simply not meant to understand some things. Bono, of U2 who is a Christian, says that his favorite song is "Amazing Grace" and his second favorite is "Help Me Make It Through the Night," and most of the time, I have to let it go at that.[59]

Perhaps these two quotes provide the best summary of what it means to live in a real world where we are willing to face the ambiguities that continue to challenge any idea of a super-simple faith.

QUESTIONS FOR REFLECTION AND CONVERSATION.

1. Are you surprised to discover that a less than perfect faith was enough for the healing of a man's son (Mark 9)?
2. Was there anything in this chapter that made for difficult reading?
3. What do you think about Buechner's reason for doubt being a part of faith?

---

59 Anne Lamott, *Plan B*, 29.

I only preach a relational theology.

When Jesus was asked to give the greatest commandment in the Law, his reply essentially combined two Hebrew Scripture passages:

> *"Love the Lord your God with all your heart and with all your soul and with all your mind." This is the first and greatest commandments. And the second is like it: "Love your neighbor as yourself." All the law and the Prophets hang on these two commandments* (Matthew 22:37-40).

In combining Deuteronomy 6:5 and Leviticus 19:18, Jesus refused to make religion solely a matter between a person and God. The Law (technically "the Law of Moses") was never intended to prescribe ways in which we could be right with God without also being right with the people around us. The greatest commandment turns out to be about all relationships: with God, with my neighbor, with myself. Healthy religion (healthy spirituality) does not ignore any of the three.

When I began my ministry and someone asked what kind of theology I had, I would reply, "I have a relational theology that encompasses the full spectrum." The questioner was usually seeking a list of things I believed (and there are things on such a list) but

I still contend that what God is most interested in for all of us is far more than correct belief. In my many different congregational experiences, I have frequently encountered those who had all their theological ducks in a row but didn't have a positive relationship with many people around them. I often wanted to ask about their theology with these three questions: How are you doing with God? How are you doing with others? How are you doing with yourself? Simplistic, yes, but plainly shifting the focus to what life is all about.

The initiative belongs to me

The crucial role of relationships was never more clearly stated than in this twist on stewardship:

> *Therefore, if you are offering your gift at the altar and there remember that your brother or sister has something against you, leave your gift there in front of the altar. First go and be reconciled to that person; then come and offer your gift* (Matthew 5:23-24).

The "therefore" in the first verse refers back to Jesus' warning against being angry with a brother or sister and, basically, attempting to bring down curses on them (my interpretation of verses 21-22). A gift should not be offered until reconciliation is completed. Does this imply that our gifts are unacceptable if we are not in a right relationship with others? It seems so with the command: "First go and make things right with that person and then you will be in a position to make an offering to God." I was always hesitant to preach a sermon on this text for fear that the offering plates would return with half the usual offerings! (Not quite true, but close.)

Where all my problems in ministry came from

As I look back over more than sixty years of pastoral ministry, it is obvious that most of my major difficulties had to do with relationships. (And at the moment I can't recall many courses in seminary that taught me how to get along with people.) Right out of the gate I had a major problem in my first church with a member who was unhappy with me because I did not measure up to the last pastor. I'll admit I didn't…and I couldn't. (Note: neither did my wife measure up to the former pastor's wife. The member bragged to me that (name withheld) was back playing the piano for the services less than two weeks after having a baby.) The real problem was I did not do a very good job in relating to him as the new pastor. His expectations were unreasonable but the failure was on my part in not knowing how to effectively deal with those expectations. I needed to work on the relationship, not on those problems.

Through the years I have read countless books on family systems and "How to Deal With Difficult People" (an actual book title). At the time of my retirement I was still working on how to better relate to people who did not find me their cup of ministerial tea. We all know we can't please everyone, but we can learn how to improve our relational skills by shifting the responsibility to ourselves. As I look back, too many times the problem was not "problem people" but the problems that were created in the way I attempted to relate to them. I learned to ask after a particularly troubling episode, "How could I have handled that differently?" Immediately, another approach surfaced and I knew something better to do the next time.

When I was at my best, I always dealt with people on a face-to-face basis. (Most of this was before the days of social media. Texting and tweeting I still view as the least effective methods of communication.) Not all conflict was resolved but at least we had a better understanding of where we each stood. The one thing I was taught was that conflict is inevitable and the goal is not conflict avoidance but conflict management (in varying forms and degrees). As in the case of Abraham and Lot, the solution may be a parting of the ways. Note: I usually had a mentor of some kind who was able to provide insight that my close-up limited vision failed to provide.

MUSINGS FROM HITHER AND YON.

It seems to be God's plan from the beginning.

> God is, I would argue, intensely relational, as seen in the
> eternal love shared by Father, Son, and Holy Spirit.[60]

Many find the doctrine of the Trinity a difficult one to understand. What is understood biblically is that God was experienced
as Father, Son, and Holy Spirit. The Bible never gives any details
of exactly how this fits together theologically. Sometimes the Spirit
is termed Holy Spirit, sometimes God's Spirit, and sometimes the
Spirit of Jesus. Jesus speaks frequently about the Father's love for
him and his love for the Father. Chris Hall in the above quote gives
the most important teaching about the Trinity: it tells us that God
is intensely relational.

If you remember, the book from which the quote is taken
records the debate Christopher Hall and John Sanders have about
the providence of God (and Calvinism). This debate has fractured
many churches and friendships. What is remarkable about this
one is not only the honesty of the arguments but the fact that the
friendship was not destroyed in the process:

> What was encouraging to both of us was that our strong
> theological disagreements never threatened our friendship, nor
> did we ever feel that friendship precluded vigorous argument
> and debate. In fact, we believe that our friendship has actually
> facilitated our ability to really listen to one another.[61]

This is not the case in many religious communities and in
many churches. *Does God Have a Future?* illustrates what healthy,
constructive dialogue is all about and underscores the need for these
kinds of discussion. One of the most telling signs of how deep their

---

60   Christopher A. Hall & John Sanders, *Does God Have a Future?*, 147.
61   Ibid, 7.

friendship is, comes at the conclusion of one of the letters from John Sanders: "Thanks for your friendship and efforts to teach me." Healthy relationships enable us to learn from one another.

A major ingredient in keeping a relationship alive.

The hardest lessons to learn in life are the ones we think we have already learned. Most people think they are good listeners, most people think that are good drivers, and most people think they are pretty good Christians. But compared to what?[62]

The above comes from a chapter titled "Learning to Listen". Matthew Kelly believes one of the ways we resist the happiness God intends for us to have is that we refuse to develop good listening habits. One of the sections in the chapter begins with this bold print heading: "Every relationship improves when we really start to listen, especially our relationship with God."[63]

I am frequently brought up short when I stop to think about what a poor job I did at listening in a particular situation. The temptation to be a "fixer" is never far below the surface. What most of us need to fix is our tendency to talk too much and listen too little!

A basic in education?

When I say that a university is a constellation of peddlers of hope, I mean to underscore three things about the work of a university. First, *education represents the regenerative capacity of our culture...*Secondly, *education harnesses the power of imagination...*Thirdly, *education is about making connections....*

---

62   Matthew Kelly, *Resisting Happiness,* 101.
63   Ibid, 103.

All real living is relating. Tear us away from our relationships with family and friends, with ideas and commitments, and there is nothing left (emphasis mine).[64]

It is obvious that I concur with Godsey, a former president of Mercer University, who, in a short collection of presidential essays, presents the essentials of a solid university education. In our present culture, I would place the essential of making connections at the top of the list.

A Strange note on which to end this section?

> As you read about my resistance, try to reflect on the times when you have met or failed to overcome it, and the times God has called you subtly or not so subtly to become the best version of yourself.[65]

Kelly believes that the way to fulfill our purpose in life — to love God and others by holy living — can best be fulfilled as we seek to become the best version of ourselves. The only observation I would make is, I know how difficult it is to relate to people who are not the best version of themselves! And that is sad because life *is* all about relationships.

QUESTIONS FOR REFLECTION AND DISCUSSION

1. What for you is one of the most important teachings in this chapter?
2. Do you believe that face to face communication remains the best way to really dialogue with others?
3. How important do you think listening is to maintaining healthy relationships?

---

64 R. Kirby Godsey, *The Courage Factor: A Collection of Presidential Essays* (Macon: Mercer University Press, 2005), 55-57.
65 Matthew Kelly, *Resisting Happiness*, 27.

CHAPTER 12:

ANGER AND FEAR CONTINUE TO BE THE GREAT MANIPULATORS

Do we know when (and how) we are being manipulated?

As the political campaigns heat up for the 2020 presidential election, the two best manipulators are much in evidence. Negative ads have won the day and the prospects for further division in our nation are on the rise. Perhaps this is the way it has always been but, today, these emotionally rousing efforts are literally in our faces and in our hands 24/7. To ask for critical thinking and rational discourse appears to be a lost cause but it continues to be the cause for those of us who are committed to something better than blowing up the bridges that connect us to one another.

A necessary sidebar: I began to wonder early on why the Scribes and Pharisees became so upset with Jesus. They were the most religious people in their day and ought to have been able to recognize a prophet when they saw one. Were they just bad people? The bottom line of their opposition appears to be Jesus' refusal to adhere to the rules and regulations that gave order and certainty to the religious life. Jesus introduced words like ambiguity, mystery, and paradox into areas they believed had long been settled. Jesus kept erasing the lines that provided the security and the assurance of identity and specific responsibilities. That's what a clear playbook does. The problem was, Jesus announced that was the wrong playbook. His teaching expanded the horizons of what obeying the Torah was all about. His was the call for critical thinking and rational discourse about matters the religious leaders were certain had already been settled.

The Bible is filled with material about anger.

If you look in a concordance, you will find an entire page devoted to anger. The dangers of anger begin early in Genesis when Abel's offering is accepted and Cain's is rejected (for what reason we are never told): *So Cain was angry, and his face was downcast* (Genesis 4:5). God confronts Cain with a suggestion and a warning: *"Why are you angry? Why is your face downcast? If you do what is right, will you not be accepted? But if you do not do what is right, sin is crouching at your door, it desires to have you, but you must rule over it"* (Genesis 4:6-7).

God never specifies just what doing right involves, but it is obvious from the narrative it has a lot to do with Cain's relationship with his brother. Although we are not given any details, jealousy and envy must have played a part. The unacceptableness of Cain's sacrifice had nothing to do with it being a produce offering instead of the animal offering presented by Abel. There was no Mosaic Law at this time and Cain was only giving an offering of what he had.

Harboring anger always keeps sin crouching at the door (sin implying what is destructive to others and to ourselves). In the very next verse, Cain invites his brother out to a field and kills him. God confronts Cain with the question, *"Where is your brother Abel?"* and Cain responds with the almost universally known response, *"Am I my brother's keeper?"* (Genesis 4:9). Anger was the motivation that led Cain to commit the first recorded murder in the Bible. He could think of no other way to deal with the rejection and humiliation that he was certain had been caused by his brother. I have a suspicion that Abel had always been the "good boy" in the family and this was the proverbial last straw.

A good question to ask.

Ephesians 4:26: *In your anger do not sin. Do not let the sun go down while you are still angry, and do not give the devil a foothold.* Surely the writer is thinking of Cain and God's warning that nursing our anger gives all of our worst instincts a foot in the door. I have finally learned to ask, "Why am I so angry with _____ or about this situation? What is in me that produces such feelings?" Owning my anger is the place to begin dealing with it. There certainly may be external causes but I am still responsible for allowing anger to rule the day.

"I have every right to be angry considering what he/she did to me?" shifts the responsibility for my anger and means it is not *my* problem. But it is. Once I own my anger, I am a long way down the path of not permitting the sun to do down while I am still in a rage. Anger is meant to be a red flag that tells me I need to pay attention to something. It should be considered a traffic light that turns red and indicates I need to stop and take stock of some things. I need to do some critical thinking and, usually, engage in some rational discourse. I repeat these two agenda items (critical thinking and rational discourse) which are so desperately needed in our culture and which will, unfortunately, have little place in the upcoming political debates because we are all more easily motivated by anger and fear than by logical discussions. The signs at marches for whatever cause are usually pithy sayings that attempt to either tap into our anger or reach down into some of our basic fears.

Jesus' most frequent commandment and his lasting gift.

Many are surprised that the most frequent command of Jesus in the Gospels is: *"Fear not."* What is also surprising to many is that the opposite of fear is not doubt, but faith — meaning trust. It is fear that keeps us agitated and irritated and afraid and it is trust that gives the gift of inner-peace. Repeating what was said earlier: this is the only place true peace can be located. If peace is based on my circumstances, any disturbance I encounter in my life (and our lives are full of these disturbances) will take that peace from me.

> (Jesus said): *Peace I leave with you, my peace I give you. I do not give to you as the world gives.* Do not let your hearts be troubled and do not be afraid (John 14:27).

John 14-16 has been called Jesus' farewell address to his disciples and the words in 14:27 represent his parting gift to them. Many have come to my office with a litany of disturbing problems and conflicts ending with the plea, "If I only could have some inner-peace." The *shalom* Jesus offers is a peace that endures in any and all circumstances if we have learned how to nurture it when all is going well. There are many reasons in our world to be afraid. These are also all reasons to accept the gift of peace and live by trust in the One who is from everlasting to everlasting and is able to keep us to and through the very end of this life.

> *From this time many of his disciples turned back and no longer followed him.*
> *"You do not want to leave too, do you?" Jesus asked the Twelve.*
> *Simon Peter answered him, "Lord, to whom shall we go? You have the words of eternal life. We have come to believe and to know that you are the Holy One of God"* (John 6:44-69).

It was not the motivation of anger and fear but the motivation of seeking the source of life, life now and life eternal, that brought this declaration from Peter. Where else can we find peace? We will never find it as a gift from anger and fear. They are not solutions or helpful ways of dealing with problems and conflicts. They are usually only doorways to hatred and violence and to the blowing up of the bridges we need to stay connected to our brothers and sisters all over the world.

MUSINGS FROM HITHER AND YON

Is this saying too much?

> Fear is the cause of every problem. It's the root of all prejudices and the negative emotions of anger, jealousy, and possessiveness. If you had no fear, you could be perfectly happy living in this world. Nothing would bother you. You'd be willing to face everything and everyone because you wouldn't have fear inside of you that could cause you disturbance.[66]

One of the best counseling techniques is to ask: "What are you afraid of?" Often this unlocks the door to the real problem and the source of the unrest the person is experiencing. To repeat: the accounts of the Incarnation and the Resurrection both have numerous "Fear not" messages for those who are confronted with events beyond their comprehension.

When God called out "Where are you?" (Genesis 3:9), Adam responded with, "I heard you walking in the Garden and I was afraid." Fear usually puts us into hiding or at least causes us to close ourselves off to life-giving experiences and relationships. Fear keeps us shut up in a very small world. Fear keeps us from stepping out and doing that which will enlarge our lives and give us purpose and meaning.

From Manipulation to Motivation.

It is a note I have kept in my file because it came from a seminary professor whom I greatly respected and was a dear friend for many years and also because it illustrates another time that has much to say to us:

> Dear Ron,
> Here is the story I first saw in *Harvard Magazine* (Vol. 86, #6, July-August 1984, p. 72): Sir Ernest Shackleton, placed an

---

66   Michael A. Singer, *The Unfettered Soul,* 73.

advertisement in *The Daily Mail* of London in 1921 in order to recruit young men for one of his Antarctic expeditions. Here is how it read:

MEN WANTED for hazardous journey. Small wages, bitter cold, long months of complete darkness, constant danger, safe return doubtful. Honour and recognition in case of success. Ernest Shackleton.

The ad generated nearly 5,000 applications.

Bringing out the best in people, challenging the highest and noblest sense of calling and purpose is no doubt why 5,000 responded. The constant appeal on the basis of anger and fear brings out the worst in us because it does not call on anything within us other than our basic instincts for survival. We respond because we feel threatened when, most of the time, the only threat is in our minds. We remember the words of president Franklin D. Roosevelt, "The only thing we have to fear is fear itself." We all needed to hear that in a time that called for the best all of us had to give. The threat of Hitler's quest for world domination was real and no baser instincts were sufficient for the fight that had to be fought.

Is it all about control?

> Who said that the way life naturally unfolds is not all right? The answer is, fear says so. The part of you inside that's not okay with itself can't face the natural unfolding of life because it's not under your control.[67]

Perhaps the reason anger and fear are such good motivators is that they alert us to persons or things that might be challenging our control in some area of our lives. How often is it heard, "He has a control issue." My thesis is that we all have control issues, and they reveal themselves if we can get in touch with the real reasons for our anger and fear. "Losing control" is one of the great fears of life. It is a great comfort in our later years of life to finally discover that we never had any real control to begin with!

---

67   Ibid, 72.

QUESTIONS FOR REFLECTION AND DISCUSSION

1. Have there been times when you were aware that someone was attempting to manipulate you by stirring up your anger and fear? How did you respond?
2. What are your strategies for not allow anger to take charge of your life?
3. Why do you think 5,000 young men responded to Shackleton's ad?

It's like looking for the fountain of youth.

"*Lost Horizon* was released in 1933 to less than an enthusiastic welcome until it won the Hawthornden Prize in 1934. Overnight it became a best-seller, and the name Shangri-La gained a permanent place in the English language." (These two sentences are from the dust jacket of the 1936 edition of James Hilton's *Lost Horizon*.)[68] A quick internet search gives this definition of *Shangri-La*: "a place regarded as an earthly paradise, especially when involving a retreat from the pressures of civilization." Some synonyms include: ecstasy, bliss, rapture, contentment, happiness, joy, felicity, seventh heaven, and cloud nine.

Shangri-La represents the yearning to return to the Garden of Eden before anything went wrong. It represents the longing for the innocence and tranquility untouched by evil, pain, suffering, conflict, and struggle. It represents the return to what, in the biblical story, was only a blip in human history. Hilton's book is a work of fiction but that has not stopped millions from yearning and searching for a time and place that is not to be found in this world. It reminds me of the search for a fountain of youth which many are convinced has got to be out there somewhere.

---

68   James Hilton, *Lost Horizon* (Cleveland: The World Publishing Company, 1936).

The only somewhere to find Shangri-La and a source for perpetual youth is in works of fiction. They simply do not exist in the world of reality with so much we feel we must eliminate in order to find that elusive "blue bird of happiness." An underlying premise behind these searches is the presumption that we were not meant to struggle with harsh realities that rob us of the peace and order we are convinced should be in our lives. Deep down we believe we were meant to live lives of ease and harmony similar to what Adam and Eve appeared to have enjoyed before the "fall" (a word which is never mentioned in the biblical text).

It's a teaching worth our understanding and consideration.

Many rabbis I have read contend that the best thing that happened to Adam and Eve is that they got thrown out of the Garden. Remaining in such a state of bliss would have literally been paradise, but Adam and Eve would never have had the opportunity to become the persons God created them to be. It was the struggles, the difficulties, the challenges, the necessary hard work, and the making of both good and bad decisions that started them on their way to a maturity beyond that of a coddled child. These rabbis hold that Eden was never meant to be the permanent home for God's supreme creation.

My reading of what went wrong in the Garden has to do with Adam and Eve attempting to gain knowledge that only belongs to God, thereby finding a way to no longer have to live as creatures in submission to a Creator. It was the grab for independence that would enable them to be their own gods. Yes, *both* of them — not just Eve as one passage of Scripture (2 Corinthians 11:3) would seem to indicate.

If most of us are honest, we know that living all our lives in a Shangri-La would not challenge us to be the kind of persons we know we are meant to be. No one likes to hear that life's greatest lessons are learned during times of hardship and adversity but deep down we know it's true. Our own times of loss and grief enable us to be a source of comfort to those who experience loss and grief. Whenever I suggest in a workshop that this world may indeed be a vale of soul-making (John Keats), the arguments against such an idea come thick and fast. John Hicks has adopted this idea as his solution to the problem of theodicy (why does a good God allow bad things to happen in his world?). This is a difficult theological pill to swallow but it is a better solution to the yet unanswered problem than many of the other solutions I have read.

What we really should be searching for.

We ought not be searching for Shangri-La but ought to be searching for better ways to meet the challenges of life with courage, faith, and hope. We ought to be searching for better ways to be compassionate and helpful to those who have been overwhelmed by life's tragedies. We ought to be searching for better ways to stand strong in a world that always seems ready to knock the props out from under us.

MUSINGS FROM HITHER AND YON

A better metaphor for where we are.

> You don't live in Mayberry, because it doesn't exist.
> The world has changed; it is tough out there, of that there can be no doubt. I am sorry to sound like a cynic, but you know I'm right.[69]

I grew up watching *The Andy Griffith Show* and never tire of seeing an occasional rerun. The fictional Mayberry became as real to most of us as any place we had ever visited. The conclusion of each episode always brought a resolution to some kind of difficulty with peace and harmony restored. Goodness reigned supreme in

---

69   Phillip C. McGraw, *Life Strategies* (New York: Hyperion, 1999), 20-21.

this world of TV comedy; you did not find the chaos and turmoil or pure evil currently reported to us on TV's nightly "breaking news." The program was almost like a weekly visit to Shangri-La.

We know the two places are myths but it does not prevent our longing — and even searching — for such places of harmony and contentment. "Dr. Phil" uses the direct approach for people who keep living in a fantasy world that prevents their dealing with reality: "We don't live in Mayberry, because it doesn't exist." We need to hear again the question God asked Adam, "Where are you?" It was no longer the reality of an innocent Eden. It was no longer Mayberry.

"You are here."

Charles Poole, in his *The Tug of Home,* tells about his experience in an extremely large hospital with multiple buildings and seemingly endless corridors. The person at the information desk gave him a map which didn't help much because of the essential missing ingredient.

> What it lacked was one of those little arrows that points to a spot and says, "You are here." So I put the map down on the information desk and said to the person, "I see where I need to go, but I don't know how to get there from here, because I'm not exactly sure where "here" is. Can you tell me where I am, right now?" She took a pencil, made a dot on the map and said, "You are here."
>
> "You are here." That phrase lands pretty near to the words that Jeremiah wrote to his friends who had been carried away captive and were living as exiles in Babylon. In his letter to the exiles, Jeremiah said, "You are here. Come to terms with the reality you face. You've bumped up against something painful that you cannot change. So you might as well live into it as fully as you can. Because, the fact is, you are here. This is your life. You are here."[70]

---

70   Charles E. Poole, *The Tug of Home* (Macon: Peake Road, 1997), 42.

Jeremiah's instructions on how to live as exiles are found in Jeremiah 29:4-11. I summarize them as counsel to throw themselves fully into life in Babylon and not to hold back. Poole gives his advice: "Whatever your family is facing, the fact is, you are here. This is your life. Wherever you are, you are here. And here, today, is where you will have to find joy, meaning and purpose if you are going to find it at all."[71] I can't imagine that the exiles in Babylon found Jeremiah's advice easy to take because he sounds so much like Dr. Phil. Jeremiah is telling the exiles: "The world has changed; it is tough out there, of that there can be no doubt. I am sorry to sound like a cynic, but you know I'm right."

Two helpful insights.

If you want to understand stress, begin by realizing that you carry around with you your own set of preconceived notions of how things should be.[72]

I can almost hear the exiles in Babylon protest: "This is not the way things are supposed to be! God promised us his protection and the city of David was meant to endure forever and how could he allow his Temple to be destroyed? This is all wrong!" They were right. It wasn't the way things should have been, but it was the new reality. They were now in a new time and a new place and it was tough.

Examining my own life and much of the stress I brought on myself, I realize I carried many preconceived notions of how things ought to be in the church and in the world. My list didn't match the realities I was facing. We cannot deal with things as they should be, we can only deal with things as they are. We cannot live in another place or another time from where we find ourselves right now. Much of my stress began to melt away when I decided to deal with things as they were, not as I imagined they should be.

---

71 Ibid, 46.
72 Michael Singer, *The Unfettered Soul,* 152.

A challenge not easily accomplished.

> (Speaking of the desert fathers and mothers): They knew
> how to mine every hardship for its spiritual gold.[73]

This does not mean simply "making the best of things" because some things don't have much "best" in them. This challenge calls for a heavy mining operation and some deep digging in order to discover the spiritual gold. Hardship may continue to be a part of our lives, but we are determined not to let it dominate our existence. We have channeled our efforts into something far more productive than the continuing search for Shangri-La.

QUESTIONS FOR REFLECTION AND CONVERSATION

1. Did anything in this chapter speak to you in a special way?
2. What do you think about the rabbis' teaching that Eden was not meant to be the permanent home for his creation?
3. Have you found ways in some hardship to mine for its spiritual gold?

---

73   Paula Huston, *Forgiveness,* 117.

Beware of "kangaroo exegesis" (jumping all over the Bible to find what you want).

If you "cherry-pick" your way through the Bible and only read passages like *The Lord is my shepherd, I shall not want,* you can avoid the most thought-provoking texts that are offered. (A typo in that line first read "cheery-pick" — which may capture the meaning even better!) When you read the Bible from cover to cover you will encounter verses that call for a wrestling match. I maintain these are some of the places in Scripture where I have learned the most and where I have learned, not so much better answers, but how to ask better questions.

Two of these tough texts are Ecclesiastes 9:11 and James 4: 13-14:

> *I have seen something else under the sun:*
> *The race is not to the swift*
> *or the battle to the strong,*
> *nor does food come to the wise*
> *or wealth to the brilliant*
> *or favor to the learned;*
> *but time and chance happen to them all.*

Now listen, you who say, "Today or tomorrow we will go to this or that city, spend a year there, carry on business and make money." Why, you do not even know what will happen tomorrow. What is your life? You are a mist that appears for a little while and then vanishes.

Uncertainty appears to be the order of the day in these oft-neglected passages of Scripture. The truth of these writings is underscored when we hear such comments as: "I never thought this could happen to me"; "It was the last thing in the world I ever planned for"; "I never imagined anything like this could ever be in my future"; "Nobody ever told me to prepare for something like this." Reality therapy is hard to take, especially when it comes from the pages of Holy Scripture, but here it is, in both the Hebrew and Christian Scriptures. The author of Ecclesiastes bases his comments on what he has seen in life. The author of James focuses his challenge on the very nature of our lives that is more "misty" than we like to believe.

The book of Job does not answer the question of why the righteous suffer.

In any workshop on Job, I always ask, "What do you believe is the central teaching of the book?" Various answers are proposed which may suggest some of the lessons to be learned but do not address the central question with which the book deals. In the Prologue, we find that strange heavenly council meeting where *the Satan* (the Hebrew indicates a title and not a proper name) makes his appearance. In the *New Living Translation,* he is called "the accuser". When the Lord asks him what he has been doing, his reply is (my paraphrase): "I've been doing my job, checking things out on the earth like I am supposed to do." God asks if he has noticed his servant Job, how good and righteous he is. The reasons for the unbelievable contest which follows is spelled out:

"Does Job fear God for nothing?" Satan replied. "HAVE YOU NOT PUT A HEDGE AROUND HIM AND HIS

HOUSEHOLD AND EVERYTHING HE HAS? (my empha-
sis). *You have blessed the work of his hands, so that his flocks and
herds are spread throughout the land. But now stretch out your
hand and strike everything he has, and he will surely curse you
to your face."*

*The Lord said to Satan, "Very well, then, everything he has
is in your power, but on the man himself do not lay a finger."*
(Job 1:9-12).

The book does not answer the question "Why do the righteous
suffer?" It does answer this Prologue question: Has God put a hedge
around those who are his? The answer is clearly, "No". Meaning:
we are subject to the same fluctuations of life, the same ups and
downs, the same adverse circumstances that all human beings face
by simply being occupants of planet earth.

Life happens to all of us.

I was once asked, "Do you think God will allow you to have a
flat tire if you are on your way to visit a person who is critically ill
and whose family has called you to come immediately?" My answer
is always, "Yes, if there happens to be a nail or glass in the road.
But he may send along a good Samaritan to help me fix the tire or
permit AAA to send help more quickly than usual." You will note
the words "he may" in my response. I never presume on what God
should do. There is no way I can manipulate God into becoming
my servant (biblically, I am his servant).

Hands go up and begin waving whenever I introduce the idea
of anything can happen to anybody. Verses come thick and fast that
God is our refuge, God is our rock, God is every watching over
us, etc. All of these are true but that does not mean that God will
put a hedge around us to protect us from life. I'm like the writer of
Ecclesiastes: I have seen too much to believe this.

God's basic pledge to us.

What I do believe is what I have come to see as *the* central teaching of Scripture: God has pledged to be with us all the way through life. He will never abandon us, and we can count on his presence, his grace, his mercy and his love. After listing a slew of bad stuff that *can* happen (and did) to many of God's people (Romans 8:35-39), Paul proclaims: *I am convinced that (nothing) will be able to separate us from the love of God that is in Christ Jesus our Lord* (vs. 39b). Psalm 23 declares that, even with our shepherd God leading us, we may have to pass through valleys as dark as death itself (something that happens to everyone). The great declaration of faith is: *I will fear no evil, for you are with me.... (vs. 4).

God does not put a hedge around us, he puts his love around us. He puts his grace around us. He puts his presence around us. That's better than a hedge any day.

MUSINGS FROM HITHER AND YON

Sometimes it does take a sledgehammer.

Parkinson's and alcohol took a sledgehammer to any illusions I may have had that I was in control.[74] (Michael J. Fox)

It ought not take anything so jarring as Parkinson's or alcohol to make us realize there is no way we can control what comes our way. "Out of the blue," and "totally unexpected" are phrases Ecclesiastes and James (in the quotes that begin the chapter) express in biblical ways to say, "We are not in control." The longer we live, the events in our lives (and in the world) convince us that "things happen." All kinds of things. Good things and bad things. Things we didn't conspire to bring about. Life keeps happening and most of it involves things we didn't plan for. In spite of all these happenings, the illusion of control dies hard.

---

74   Michael J. Fox, *Always Looking Up*, 201.

The cure for worry over lack of control?

> Your inner growth is completely dependent upon the re-
> alization that the only way to find peace and contentment is
> to stop thinking about yourself. You're ready to grow when
> you finally realize that the "I" who is always talking inside will
> never be content.[75]

The desire to control, the desire to keep things manageable, is
all about me. It is about what I want and what I believe will make
for the kind of world in which I will be happy. In the New Testament Jesus talks about "denying self" which means nothing less
than taking ourselves off center stage. When everything is all about
me, I can count on being almost constantly upset over difficulties
in every area of my existence. Getting the focus off self is especially
important whenever life does throw us a curve.

Michael J. Fox writes: "For whatever reason, I had been spared
the torture of depression."[76] He does confess bouts of sadness, fear,
and anxiety. You don't have to read very far in his book to know
one of the reasons he escaped the paralysis of deep depression that
often comes with Parkinson's: Fox does not keep thinking about
himself; he thinks about his family and the increasing number of
those who suffer from Parkinson's and what he can do to aid in
research to deal with the symptoms of this disease.

"Why is this happening to me," "what did I do to deserve this,"
and "life just isn't fair," are all phrases we might justifiably use in a
moment of extreme frustration over our situation. As a stance for
facing our difficulties, these are not helpful strategies. Years ago,
I heard an illustration about an orchestra that was tuning up for
a concert. One player seemed to be out of sync; he simply kept
playing the same note over and over again. When the conductor
confronted him about his technique the reply was, "Oh, these other
players are looking for the right note. I have found it." The teller of
that story then added: "And the note was not 'do'; it was not 're';

75 Michael A. Singer, *The Unfettered Soul*, 15.
76 Michael J. Fox, *Always Looking Up*, 26.

it was 'mi,' 'mi,' 'mi'!" Repeatedly played, that is the note that will create disharmony within yourself and with everyone else.

It is in harmony with the title of Fox's book.

> No matter what happens below you, just turn your eyes upward and relax your heart.[77]

Although not in the same context as Michael J. Fox's philosophy, this quote illustrates the same truth. *Always Looking Up: The Adventures of an Incurable Optimist* is the prescription Fox found for a life that kept him from despair. My prescription would be the same with this different slant: *Always Looking Up: The Adventures of an Incurable Faith in the Love and Faithfulness of God* — no matter what happens! If you are like Jacob of old who wanted to make a covenant with God, and began it with "If you will do this, then I will promise to...." (Genesis 28:20f), then there is no way you will always be looking up. And that is the only place to look in a world where anything can happen to anybody.

QUESTIONS FOR REFLECTION AND CONVERSATION

1. How do you interpret the verses from Ecclesiastes and James?
2. Do you agree that God does not put a hedge around us?
3. How do you feel about Michael J. Fox's philosophy as expressed in the title of his book and the variation suggested above?

---

77   Michael A. Singer, *The Unfettered Soul,* 78.

It shows up early in the Bible and is present throughout all of its pages.

The closest the Bible comes to providing an answer to the question of theodicy, (why does a good God allow such bad things to happen to people?), is that there is another force at work in the world. It is a force that is at odds with the purposes and plans of God. It is the force of evil. That force is nameless until we get to the Christian Scriptures when we find it personified in Satan. (Remember: in the book of Job "the Satan" is a title and not a proper name). Things hardly get underway before evil raises its ugly head in the form of a serpent in the Garden with one of the biggest temptations: "You can't really trust God. He doesn't really want what's best for you. This restriction he has placed on you plainly reveals he's holding out on you." Evil quickly reaches another level when Cain kills his brother Abel.

Somewhere I read about a pastor's class where boys and girls were asked, "If all the bad people in the world were green and all the good people were purple, what color would you be?" One youngster immediately spoke up, "I'd be streaky!" The reality is: we are all streaky people. We often find ourselves being like the person in the nursery rhyme: "Jump! Jump! I'm little jumping Joan. When I'm good, I'm very, very good. And when I'm bad, I'm horrid!" We are all capable of so much good and, yet, there is a darker side, a shadow side, to our natures that frightens us. "I just wasn't my best self today," is something we all have said. We could have said, "I was my streaky self today."

Hitting us when and where we are most vulnerable.

Immediately following Jesus' baptism and prior to the inauguration of his public ministry, we are told that the devil leads him into the wilderness (desert) where satan attempts to persuade him to launch a ministry totally different from the one Jesus is convinced is his calling. Only Luke tells us: *When the devil had finished all this tempting, he left him until an opportune time* (4:13). Just as with Cain, evil was lurking in the shadows waiting for a moment of weakness to launch another attack.

Ephesians describes the perennial battle with evil like this:

> *Finally, be strong in the Lord and in his mighty power. Put on the full armor of God, so that you can take your stand against the devil's schemes. For our struggle is not against flesh and blood, but against the rulers, against the authorities, against the powers of this dark world and against the spiritual forces of evil in the heavenly realms* (6:10-12).

What follows is the description of the armor which we are to put on: the belt of truth, the breastplate of righteousness, the sandals of the gospel of peace, the shield of faith, the helmet of salvation, and the sword of the Spirit (verses 14-17). This armor is to be worn *so that when the day of evil comes, you may be able to stand your ground, and after you have done everything, to stand* (6:13). The writer does not say *if the day of evil comes* but *when* it comes. The basic assumption of Scripture is that evil is a reality, and we had better be ready to meet it when it makes its appearance.

Advance readiness is the best preparation.

It is not a game plan to begin to look for our armor when evil is breaking down the door. The armor is not described as something which can be put on quickly. Truth, righteousness, peace, faith, salvation, and the Spirit all speak of intangibles beyond our own ability to make. These are all gifts from God that are acquired through desire, prayer, discipline, and remaining enrolled as a student in God's continuing education classes. Each of the six parts of our armor is really an attribute that is part of what we call the spiritual life. Evil is so vast, so destructive, so powerful, so pervasive that sometimes the best we can do is to remain standing after its onslaught. The total elimination of that evil is not promised until the book of Revelation describes a great battle after which it is no more.

The perennial questions: why doesn't God do something about that evil now? Why doesn't he step into the battle and defeat those forces that are opposed to all he is trying to accomplish in our world? I have no answer except that in the meantime we are to be his warriors against everything that is destructive to humanity and is attempting to thwart God's will being done on earth as it is in heaven. This is no game where most of the people are spectators sitting in the bleachers. We are all on the playing field and the opposing team doesn't play by any rules. It is demonic in its intentions and in its methods. That is why the gear we are to wear is the armor described in Ephesians.

Courage and faith remain forever linked.

Even as I write, the news is filled with terrorists' shootings and bombings. While not as vast or destructive as the Holocaust, it still represents anger, hatred, and vengeance. After the most recent shooting at a synagogue, the Rabbi (who was wounded in the attack) made a brief speech in which he said in essence, "We will not stay down! We will not be defeated! We are still standing!" Our obligation is, of course, to stand with such people and do all in our power to strive for a culture that stops sowing the seeds of anger, fear, and resentment. Walking with the sandals of peace on our feet implies that every step we take, every action of our lives, will perpetuate the *shalom* that Jesus left us as his parting gift. We are to leave the trail of peace everywhere we have walked.

Evil is a reality. But it is not the only reality. Love, mercy, goodness, beauty, truth, forgiveness, grace, and possibility are also real. We are meant to live in a world of reality, but we need to make certain our lives reflect another dimension of reality — the dimension that one day will be the only reality.

MUSINGS FROM HITHER AND YON

We still have problems accepting the reality of evil.

> Alan Watts: "By and large Western civilization is a cele- bration of the illusion that good may exist without evil, light without darkness, and pleasure without pain, and this is true of both its Christian and secular technological phases."[78]

Unfortunately, I found this to be true both inside and outside the church. It seems as though the piece of folk wisdom, "If you want the rainbow you've got to have the rain," has been forgotten. We certainly find good and light and pleasure in our world. But these are not unmixed blessings. Evil, darkness, and pain are always intruding into our lives. To deny these is similar to the denial of the shadow side that exists in all of us. (Example: David, even as a man after God's own heart, had a shadow side dark enough for the entrance of adultery and murder).

---

78   Richard Rohr, *The Naked Now,* 143.

These realities ought to rule out simplicity.

Randy Alcorn: "I don't appreciate neat and tidy responses to suffering."[79]

There is just too much suffering, pain, and disability in our world to permit neat and tidy responses. These usually are the defensive weapons of those who fear confronting the harsh reality and the depth of the darkness that keeps attempting to dim the light of faith and hope. Complexity is the order of the day in the world and in the life of faith. Simplicity is not an adequate response to anything.

Three views on evil.[80]

1. Pantheism *affirms* God and *denies* evil.
2. Atheism *affirms* evil and *denies* God.
3. Theism *affirms* both God and evil.

Norman Geisler, who takes a conservative approach to the question of evil, has given these three basic categories for discussion. Most who read this book will take the theistic approach, affirming both God and evil which brings us back to the title of Geisler's book, *If God, Why Evil?* I have yet to read a book that gives an answer that covers all the bases. The first two views need little further discussion but the third view opens Pandora's box.

Two quotes that provide some direction.

God transformed evil. He did not abolish it.
Evil can't be undone, only purged and redeemed.[81]

---

79 Larry J. Waters and Roy B. Zuck, eds., *Why God?: Suffering and Disability in the Bible and Church* (Wheaton: Crossway, 2011), 9.
80 Norman L. Geisler, *If God, Why Evil?* (Minneapolis: Bethany House, 2011), 12.
81 Larry J. Waters and Roy B. Zuck, eds., *Why God?*, 54, 56.

The only suggestion about the abolishment of evil is in the final wrap-up of things in the book of Revelation (which presents another whole set of exegetical challenges). There is much in the Bible about the transformation of evil into something that brings about the true purpose and plan of God for his world and the persons in it.

The suggestion that evil can't be undone but only purged and redeemed seems to be borne out in Scripture and in life. Jesus casts out evil spirits and confronts the demonic in a world that acknowledged it was filled with both. It has always been of interest to me that when Jesus stills the storm on Lake Galilee, he uses the same words he uses when he performs an exorcism. The biggest word I would use for what occurs in Scripture and what should occur in life is "redeemed." A situation is reclaimed, redirected, and renewed. Life is able to continue in another direction (often not without some remaining scars from the past) that only be described as a transformation.

1 Peter 5:8-9 underscores the reality of evil and how it needs to be met:

> *Be alert and of sober mind. Your enemy the devil prowls around like a roaring lion looking for someone to devour. Resist him, standing firm in the faith, because you know that your fellow believers throughout the world are undergoing the same kind of sufferings.*

The reality of evil is clearly recognized here and its power is underscored. In the biblical world, to compare it with a hungry roaring lion is the call to take the danger seriously. A bowl of warm milk and a calm, "Here kitty, kitty," is not a sufficient response to this kind of reality.

C. S. Lewis…understood that we are still living in "enemy-occupied territory." Spiritual evil still roams the world, and it is much stronger than we are in our merely natural state. We need to become tougher.[82]

---

82   Paula Huston, *Forgiveness*, 119.

QUESTIONS FOR REFLECTION AND CONVERSATION

1. What problems do you have with some of the concepts in this chapter?
2. What ideas spoke to you about how best to handle the manifestations of evil in our world?
3. Do you believe that courage and faith must always be linked?

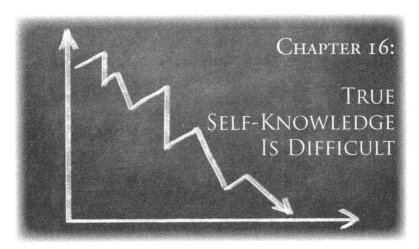

About the time I think I know myself, I deal myself another surprise.

"To know thyself is the beginning of wisdom." Almost everyone knows these words from the ancient Greek philosopher Socrates (c. 470-399). It is a high calling and a noble achievement, not because it is impossible but because it requires a lifetime of soul-searching.

One of Jesus' parables illustrates just how difficult knowing ourselves really is.

> *Two men went up to the Temple to pray, one a Pharisee and the other a tax collector. The Pharisee stood by himself and prayed: "God I thank you that I am not like other people — robbers, evildoers, adulterers — or even like this tax collector. I fast twice a week and give a tenth of all I get."*
>
> *But the tax collector stood at a distance. He would not even look up to heaven, but beat his breast and said, "God, have mercy on me a sinner"* (Luke 18:10-13).

The context of this parable reveals a man who was confident of his own righteousness and looked down on everyone else. This is Luke's explanation for Jesus telling the story (vs. 9). He stood by himself; he felt entitled to draw close to God in contrast to the tax collector who stood at a distance. His "righteousness" gave him full access in prayer. The tax collector did not even look up (the usual stance in prayer) which the Pharisee evidently did. The Pharisee's prayer was one of self-congratulation, the prayer of the other one of contrite confession. The Pharisee couldn't really see anything he lacked in the exercise of his religion but for the tax collector his failings and unworthiness were all too evident.

As with most parables, there is a turning upside down of things when Jesus concludes that the tax collector, rather than the Pharisee, *went home justified by God* (vs. 14a). Meaning: he went home in a right relationship with God and the Pharisee just went home. Why? Jesus explained: *All those who exalt themselves will be humbled, and those who humble themselves will be exalted* (vs. 14b). The Pharisee's exaltation resulted in his inability to really know himself. He honestly didn't believe he had anything to confess, much less to be ashamed of. He stood head and shoulders above the riff-raff (and he did!). He observed the laws of his faith but was unable to see his pride and arrogance. He couldn't see any problem with a faith that distanced him from those he deemed "unworthy." He had forgotten Hosea 6:6: *I desire mercy, not sacrifice.* He did not recognize this void in his religious life.

It is so much easier to see you than it is to see myself.

> *"Why do you look at the speck of sawdust in someone else's eye and pay no attention to the plank in your own eye?"* (Matthew 7:3).

Because I have a plank in my eye, I'm unable to see very clearly; but even with that limitation I usually have "speck-tacular" vision! The plank is not in my line of sight. Self-knowledge is challenging and frequently humiliating. It brings us down to the level of common humanity where all other people exist. Knowing ourselves begins with the recognition that this is our first obligation in the pursuit of wisdom, not the ability to be God's "private eye" pointing out the missteps of others. To know ourselves is a duty, an obligation, a necessity both in our relationships with others and our relationship with God.

Gert Behanna once spoke to a pastors' conference with such wit and condor that a recording was made of her presentation. Speaking to clergy, she opened with: "When the Bible tells us that *all have sinned and fall short of the glory of God,* I presume this includes you." There is a space of silence on the recording and then the laughter begins. Our self-knowledge necessarily begins with this recognition. Behanna told about her battle with alcohol and drugs: "The good thing about being an alcoholic is that when you fall down drunk you will know it, or someone will be kind enough to tell you. However, when I graduated to the Christian sins, I found these much more difficult to deal with. Am I proud of not being proud? Do I look down on people who look down on people?" She continued with this litany of "Christian sins" that are always difficult to acknowledge.

Gert Behanna gave a wakeup call to too many of us who unconsciously thank God that we are not like other people and thereby blind ourselves to the kind of people we really are. AA meetings are a great reminder for all of us. Each person who speaks must begin with, "I'm _____ and I'm an alcoholic." No past tense bragging about overcoming but a present tense confession of an ongoing battle. Self-knowledge is not the call for confessing that we are less than children of God, those created in his image, but the recognition that we are vulnerable and prone to self-congratulations more than honest self-reflection.

The need for a faith community and/or a support group.

The difficulty of honest self-reflection is one of the reasons we all need a faith community that is loving and accepting but that also challenges us to see parts of ourselves blocked by our "plank vision." Many seek a spiritual advisor who, more often than not, simply listens and asks questions that we need to hear and have not thought to ask ourselves. I have often wondered if judgment day might not be that time when, instead of an angel reading off a list of "charges" against us, we suddenly see ourselves as we really are. Perhaps I'd better get ready for such a possibility by continuing and deepening my efforts at knowing myself. (I am trusting that this self-knowledge will come in small doses!)

MUSINGS FROM HITHER AND YON

It's the only word to use.

In discussing human behavior in his over seven-hundred-page book, Robert Sapolski summarizes everything in a single sentence in the epilogue: "If you had to boil this book down to a single phrase, it would be 'It's complicated.'" These are words of a neuroscientist and primatologist who has done extensive research and incredible analysis of the science of human behavior. This is one of the observations on the final page of endorsements in the front of the book: "Read Robert Sapolsky's marvelous book *Behave* and you'll never again be surprised by the range and depth of our own bad behavior."[83]

This kind of carefully researched information ought to make us very hesitant to judge the motives and reasons for another's behavior (as well as our own!). From a book dealing with emotions in the workplace:

> Effective emotional knowledge demands a profound level of *self-reflection,* an active imagination, and an ability not only to envision alternate approaches to a given situation but also to understand that there are entire invisible galaxies of salient emotional facts behind almost every workplace exchange.[84]

---

83   Robert Sapolsky, *Behave,* unnumbered page.
84   Anne Kreamer, *It's Always Something* (New York: Random House, 2011), 15.

At the end of that paragraph I wrote: "same for the church." This is not a negative statement; it is simply a corrective to the supposition that when people come to church they leave those galaxies of emotional facts at the door. I can testify I have been in meetings where I have actually seen those "galaxies of salient emotions" swirling around! We are all human beings with a complexity that too many have not yet discovered.

It becomes highly personal.

> I realized I had to set aside a professional identity (which can be a mask behind which to hide emotionally)....I focused on the need for honesty....I became less disturbed about discovering other people's thoughts about me and more concerned about better understanding myself....None of this came easy.[85]

Too many in public life (and that includes those of us in ministry) rely far too much on what others are saying about us to measure how we are doing. This used to be called being "other-directed" as opposed to being "inner-directed." The Gospels clearly illustrate that Jesus resisted the evaluations of the crowd and their concepts of what he ought to be doing (many were ready to crown him king and take on the Roman empire). I was taught in many seminary classes the need to listen to the inner voice of God's Spirit in conjunction with the inner voice of our spirit as the final step in seeking any kind of guidance. It's also the major step in getting to know ourselves. If we're always "playing to the house," we'll never get a chance to know ourselves in any depth.

> Knowing yourself is having a good relationship with yourself, so you know your own emotions, fears, motivations, doubts, and aspirations. It also means knowing that we are always creating the story of who we are and recognizing the impermanent and ephemeral nature of this story.[86]

85 Ibid, 22-23.
86 Marc Lesser, *Know Yourself, Forget Yourself* (New York: MJF Books, 2013), 71.

These two observations make self-knowledge highly personal. We need to have a good relationship with ourselves (for most of us this is not an easy matter as we often tend to be far too judgmental toward ourselves). We need to recognize that we are always in the process of creating the story of who we are. I think of just how many times and just how much the story of who I am has changed in my eighty-four years.

(Sidebar: My reviewer suggested that some who read this book may find it difficult to walk from "know thyself" to "have a good relationship with yourself." I believe the bridge between these two is the reliance on God's grace and his total acceptance of us just as we are. Other sections in this book attempt to speak to these crucial issues that link the two seemingly opposite positions.)

QUESTIONS FOR REFLECTION AND CONVERSATION

1. Did anything in this chapter strike you in a personal way?
2. How do you feel about the need for a faith community or a support group to help you get to know yourself better?
3. Have you ever felt those galaxies of salient emotional facts swirling around you?

Thankfully, grace has always had the first word, and will ultimately have the last word.

When one of my congregation greeted me following the service with, "You preach a lot on grace, don't you?" my response was: "What else is there?" Ephesians 2:8 is a frequently quoted verse but I always insist on attaching the prelude which begins in verse 4:

> *But because of his great love for us, God, who is rich in mercy, made us alive with Christ even when we were dead in transgressions — it is by grace you have been saved. And God raised us up with Christ and seated us with him in the heavenly realms in Christ Jesus, in order that in the coming ages he might show the incomparable riches of his grace, expressed in his kindness to us in Christ Jesus. For it is by grace you have been saved, through faith — and this is not from yourselves, it is the gift of God — not of works, so that no one can boast* (Ephesians 2:4-9).

"Justification by grace through faith" was not only the watchword of the Reformation, it is the phrase G. K. Chesterton once called "the furious love of God."[87] I cannot think of a better description of God's love for us. The Ephesians text explodes with superlatives about this love: *his great love for us, rich in mercy, incom-*

---

87 Brennan Manning, *The Ragamuffin Gospel* (Sisters, OR: Multnomah Publishers, 2000), 22.

parable riches of his grace, the gift of God. No one ever exemplified that love better than Jesus of Nazareth in his words and ministry.

What really got Jesus into trouble.

I once heard a radio sermon in which the minister asked, "Why did Jesus get into so much trouble? I'll tell you why — because he preached against sin!" As I read the gospels, it is more than evident that Jesus got into major trouble for associating with sinners, and offering God's forgiveness as though there was an endless supply (which there is!). If anything, he was judged much too soft on sin in general and certain sins in particular. He became known as the friend of sinners because his was not the judgmental approach of the religious leaders of the day but one that spoke acceptance even to the most unacceptable.

My basic definition of grace is the total love and acceptance of God for each of us exactly as we are. Many of us have difficulty accepting that acceptance. Surely there is some deed to be done, some sacrifice to be offered, some penance to be performed, some prayer to be spoken before we can receive that acceptance. According to the Ephesians text, this is a gift of God — his great gift to all of us right now, this moment, before we do any cleaning up of our act. That will follow later as our response to God's grace and love and our desire to be more of what he has placed within us to be. My watchword about salvation is: Salvation is all of grace, and ethics is all of gratitude. How can we not seek to be better people, to live more as God's Kingdom people, not in order to earn anything but in thanksgiving for what we have already received?

You'll have to read it to believe it.

Brennan Manning's last book is *All is Grace*. A printed endorsement in the book probably comes as quite a shock to an unsuspecting reader: "Initially I was confused, wondering how Brennan could preach a powerful message of grace but live a powerless life of chronic alcoholism....I learned the truth of the gospel from Brennan, the same gospel you will find in this book: that in the end, my sin will never outweigh God's love."[88] Three quotes from Brennan answer the question the reader asks:

> But if I'm learning anything about the world of grace, it's that failure is always chance for a do-over.[89]

> If asked whether I am fully letting God love me, just as I am, I would answer, "No, but I'm trying."[90]

> My message unchanged for more than fifty years is this: *God loves you unconditionally, as you are and not as you should be, because nobody is as they should be. It is the message of grace....*[91]

Brennan has never succeeded in conquering his alcohol addiction. It is a continuing battle in his life. How can an alcoholic preach the gospel? Read this book and you will find out. Although it does seem to me that even Paul speaks about ministers as imperfect vessels who are used by God anyway! 2 Corinthians 4:7 in the King James Version is: *We have this treasure in earthen vessels.* The TNIV reads: *We have this treasure in jars of clay to show that this all-surpassing power is from God and not from us.*

We need to get off of God's payroll and into his blessing plan.

To cease trying to earn God's grace, love, and forgiveness and acknowledge that these come only as God's gifts, is the first step in claiming the freedom Jesus said he came to bring us. It is the freedom that enables us to live creatively, redemptively, and

---

88   Brennan Manning, *All is Grace* (Colorado Springs: David C. Cook, 2011), 19.
89   Ibid, 162.
90   Ibid, 184.
91   Ibid, 192.

non-judgmentally. Because we feel accepted just as we are, we can begin to offer that same acceptance to others — just as they are. "If only he would;" "If only I could persuade her to stop;" "If only there wasn't this irritating personal trait." These are only a fraction of the litanies that continue to keep personal relationships fragile and fractured. "I will accept you only when you become more acceptable" is not going to elicit the response, "I'll do whatever is necessary." It may result in a simple "Goodbye." (I am not talking about tolerating abusive behavior of any kind. That is totally unacceptable and is a matter for immediate counseling or legal action.)

When I think back on one word that has described my faith journey, the only one that comes to mind is *grace*. Just at the right time, in the just the right way, and in the right measure, God has provided the gifts that enabled me to continue my journey. This, is spite of poor decisions on my part and many missteps. As I look back over my life, the questions I most often ask myself are: "Why did I do that? Why didn't I do a better job at that? What was I thinking of?" Rather than wallow in guilt (which I have done), I finally got some good advice about the regrets that inevitably fill our lives: the very fact that I now recognize so many mistakes and poor decisions in my life shows that I am no longer that person. I have grown some in my understanding and, yes, in wisdom.

When I look back over my life, my conclusion is a simple one: It has been grace all the way and I'm counting on that grace to lead me all the way home.

MUSINGS FROM HITHER AND YON

Do many of us secretly feel that way?

The contemporary preacher Fred Craddock once tinkered with details of the parable to make (a) point. In a sermon, he had the father slip the ring and robe on the *elder* brother, then kill the fatted calf in honor of his years of faithfulness and obedience. A woman in the back of the sanctuary yelled out, "That's the way it *should* have been written!"[92]

The reason it doesn't seem fair that the party was thrown for the younger brother instead of the older brother is because it isn't fair! If grace were about fairness it wouldn't be grace. I have been asked in workshops, "How would you feel if you had been in the place of the older brother?" We need to examine how we feel about the undeserved "rewards" lavished on the prodigal and only a "Come join the party" for the faithful son.

The Pharisees, who were complaining that Jesus associated and ate with tax collectors and sinners, felt he was fraternizing with the wrong crowd. To respond to their criticism, Jesus tells three stories in Luke 15. The first is about a lost sheep, the second is about a lost coin, and the third is about a lost son. The first two stories end with a party because the sheep and the coin have been found. A party is certainly appropriate. The elder brother represents those who resent a party being thrown for a lost son who returns home with not even a rebuke for his outrageous behavior.

The parable has no title in the text (as do none of Jesus' parables) but is told to illustrate the nature of grace. It is outrageous because it is totally undeserved and goes against every teaching that we reap exactly what we have sown. Here a young man sows wild oats and reaps a banquet. What cannot be ignored is what precedes the return: the confession, "Father, I have sinned against heaven and against you. I am no longer worthy to be called your son; make me like one of your hired servants." The son gets out only the first two parts of his confession before the father commands the servants to bring a robe, a ring, and sandals for him.

---

92 Philip Yancey, *What's So Amazing About Grace?* (Grand Rapids: Zondervan Publishing, 1997), 54.

How is such a welcome possible?

> God does not love us because we are good. God loves us
> because God is good. That changes everything.[93]

Many have observed that a more suitable title for the parable
would be "The Parable of the Waiting Father". It is the father who
continues to watch for the return of his son, finally sees him "a long
way off," and runs to meet him. Here are the keys to the parable. It
has nothing to do with "fairness" but with the love of the father for
his son regardless of how far away he strayed. It has everything to
do with the father's love and nothing to do with the son's behavior.
The very fact that he decided to come home with the realization
of how foolish and destructive his journey into the "far country"
had been and how little he deserves from his father was all that was
necessary on his part.

Jesus tells another parable in which workers wait in the mar-
ketplace to be hired for the day to work in a vineyard (Matthew
20). Some are hired at 6:00 a.m. (the beginning of the work day),
and others progressively at 9:00, noon, 3:00, and 5:00 p.m. When
the workers line up to be paid, those who came at 5:00 are paid
first and receive a full day's wage. Everyone else receives the same.
Those who put in long hours express their resentment that those
who worked only one hour received as much as they did. The owner
responds with, "Are you envious because I'm so generous?"

This story is not about labor relations but about the nature of
grace. It has no bearing on what one deserves, much less on what
one has "earned." If you earn it, it is not grace!

The note on which to end.

> During a British conference on comparative religions,
> experts from around the world debated what, if any, belief was
> unique to the Christian faith. They began eliminating possi-
> bilities. Incarnation? Other religions had different versions of

---

93   Richard Rohr, *The Naked Now*, 79.

gods appearing in human form. Resurrection? Again, other religions had accounts of return from death. The debate went on for some time until C.S. Lewis wandered into the room. "What's the rumpus about?" he asked, and heard in reply that his colleagues were discussing Christianity's unique contribution among world religions. Lewis responded, "Oh, that's easy. It's grace."[94]

QUESTIONS FOR REFLECTION AND CONVERSATION

1. Do you think "the furious love of God" is a good description of grace?
2. How do you feel about Brennan Manning's confession?
3. Do you see yourself on God's payroll or in his blessing plan?

---

94   Philip Yancey, *What's So Amazing About Grace?*, 45.

CHAPTER 18:

CHANGE
IS INEVITABLE

A bumper sticker: "Change is good. You go first."

My dad often commented how much the world had changed in his lifetime. He saw his first automobile as a youngster and lived to see a man set foot on the moon. If he were alive today, my comment would be, "That was only the beginning!" No generation has ever experienced such rapidity of change as we have and that change has not been limited to one field — it has been comprehensive. It seemed a science fiction dream when, in a daily comic strip, Dick Tracy talked on his two-way wrist radio. Hardly anyone envisioned the day when we could press a button on our cell phone and talk to anyone, anywhere in the world.

Our world has exploded with innovations and achievements in electronics that have made the science fiction dreams of the past current realities. We literally have the world at our fingertips (and carry it in our pockets). Instant communication is a reality and seen by many as a necessity. (The debate on just how effective that communication is as opposed to face to face conversation continues to rage.) Advancements in medical procedures have enabled many of us to remain active into later years that in earlier days would have meant rocking chairs.

The information explosion continues to overwhelm us because it keeps coming faster than we can process it. The old *Dragnet* line, "Just the facts, ma'am, just the facts" is what we now get. The analyzing and interpretation of those "facts" has taken a backseat to the accumulation of more data. Big questions are ignored: How much information do we really need? Is the accumulation of facts the same as acquiring wisdom? How much time can I give to checking out Facebook and the internet without sacrificing other more relevant demands?

The world that is no more.

Much of the change has been good but much of it has left us floundering in a sea of information and at a loss for the real tools of communication that came from the human voice and pen and ink. (I am told no one writes thank you notes any more but simply sends emails. Many no longer send Christmas cards but subscribe to a service that enables them to send clever animated ecards. This list goes on.) Our heritage is rich because we are blessed with the correspondence of so many of history's remarkable people. I recently read a book based on the letters between Galileo and his daughter. To listen to these voices from the past is to bring an understanding of that past that even an excellent biography is unable to do. Where would we be if they had only emailed or texted one another? That sounds like a Luddite, but I always assure people I'm not one (but I'm close!).

The world in which my wife and I grew up is no more. That's what happens when you live into your eighties as I'm certain it has always happened — but not to the same extent and not with the same speed. Many years ago, I was doing a workshop for some college students and I commented how my world was different. I told them that often as a college student, on a Saturday night many of us would gather in the student lounge to watch the *Perry Como Show*. A hand immediately went up and the question came, "Who was Perry Como?" I explained in a civil tone instead of giving my preferred response, "He was someone who could actually sing!" But that would have been unfair, unkind, and untrue. The music today is a different style, for a different time, for people who grew up listening to different songs.

The reason we grieve when things change.

Many books have been written on how best to deal with change, but the piece of wisdom that sticks with me is this one: "All change is experienced as loss, even if it is good change." Change means something new has replaced something that used to be (I chose not to use the word "old" which implies "out of date" and I am not persuaded that everything in the past is out of date). We know we cannot hold on to the past, that we can never bring back what used to be, although in areas of music I still have a pretty good CD collection and as a movie buff, a substantial collection of DVDs. Some have said I can wallow in nostalgia any time I want. I don't see it that way. I consider it a way to enjoy some of the classic things of my earlier life. What's wrong with listening to Nat King Cole, Frank Sinatra, Louis Armstrong, good jazz, or even big band music? Thanks to SeriusXM radio I am now able to enjoy these and many more as I drive. What's wrong with being able to watch: *The Sound of Music, Fiddler on the Roof, Ben Hur, All Quiet on the Western Front,* any of the Alfred Hitchcock films, Fred Astaire and Ginger Rogers classics, and other classics that seem to be just as fresh as when they were made? I always loved action movies like the *Indiana Jones* series and *Star Wars,* but so many films today seem to be overwhelmed with special effects and action in the form of violence. Even in action movies, I look for a good story, good character development, and some good lessons to take away in the end. I suppose that makes me about as old-fashioned as you can get.

The only place we have to live.

This is not to reject what is good and wholesome and helpful in the new world in which I now find myself. Change is inevitable and this is now the world that is. I can choose to live in no other.

This sounds like common sense but it is not easily achieved. In one of my books I have a chapter titled, "There Are No Trains to Yesterday." Even though many still wait at Hopeful Station for one to show up, the waiting is in vain. We can only rejoice for all the good in the past and commit ourselves to living fully in the present that is now the only place to invest our lives. The worst thing we can do is to spend our time complaining about how things are today while maintaining that everything was so much better in the past. To begin with, it wasn't. The "Good Old Days" were never as good as we imagine them. Our memories are very selective and the further we get from past experiences the better they look. If I'm honest, I think I did a generous amount of complaining even then.

If we intend to relate effectively to people around us, we have to live present- tense lives. As we age, the temptation is to spend too much of our time reminiscing and too little of our time appreciating the opportunities that now belong to us. The world will never be exactly what any of us want. Why should we expect things to be tailor-made to our likes and dislikes? Earlier we looked at Ecclesiastes 9:11 with its startling *time and chance happen to them all.* We could just as easily render this verse: *change and chance happen to them all.* It's a moving world. Today, an extremely fast-moving one. Time doesn't stand still and neither does anything else. Change is built into the essence of the universe. I must learn to live with that and seek to be a part of what is best, seek to address what seems to be corrosive, and, in many ways, learn to go with the flow because change is inevitable.

MUSINGS FROM HITHER AND YON

"Change, we discovered the hard way, is a process, not an event."[95]

Joan Chittister writes about the changes that came to the religious order to which she belongs with an honesty, openness, and

95   Joan Chittister, *The Way We Were* (New York: Orbis Books, 2005), 126.

faith that can be applied to any changes we face, organizationally or personally. The discovery that change is a process and not an event came the hard way. The other thing that came the hard way for me is the truth of these lines from her book:

> There is no such thing, social scientists know now, as "controlled change." Change is a dynamic that builds a coherent future out of a chaotic present.[96]

My desire to control change, both culturally and in the church, has only brought added frustration. Again, I learned the hard way:

> Change can be viewed as either exciting or frightening, but regardless of how we view it, we must all face the fact that change is the very nature of life. If you have a lot of fear, you won't like change. You'll try to create a world around you that is predictable, controllable, and definable.[97]

Who doesn't like the words predictable, controllable, and definable? These words put us in charge. And isn't that where we all want to be? The chapter in which Singer gives the above quote is titled "let go now or fall" (his chapter titles are all in lower case). We keep coming back to mastering the art of letting go as the basic essential in any spirituality.

Knowing when to accept and when to drive change.

Marc Lesser lets us know just how challenging the material in his book will be by the title, *Know Yourself, Forget Yourself.* Paradox is built into every chapter: "Be Confident, Question Everything"; "Embrace Emotion, Embody Equanimity"; "Benefit Others, Benefit Yourself"; and the chapter from which the heading for this unit comes: "Fight for Change, Accept What Is." From that chapter:

---

96 Ibid, 181.
97 Michael A. Singer, *The Unfettered Soul*, 71.

To be effective requires knowing when to practice acceptance and when to drive change. This is more difficult than it
sounds.[98]

It sounds so difficult to me that I wrote "Amen!" in the margin.
It calls to mind the Serenity Prayer of AA which is also more difficult than it sounds. It calls for our reflection and deep thinking in
conjunction with others who have the patience to deal with issues
that require a great deal of space and time. This is an area that was
a source of continuing anxiety in working with churches. Some
have the motto (unspoken), "Come weal or come woe, our status
is quo." Stated in other terms: "We shall not be moved." Others in
the congregation were "makers and shakers" who believed things
could never remain as they were but called for constant renovation
and improvisation. Keeping these two groups in dialogue with one
another was not an easy task; the lines between acceptance and
when to drive change were not always clear.

One thing that makes it so difficult.

> My friend spoke and said my losses have been many, cu-
> mulative, and varied, which frequently happens during our
> later years. They have called for different responses, but she
> suspected their very frequency probably has not allowed me
> time to absorb, process them. Loss always depletes and wearies
> us, she said; and when we have to store our losses up inside,
> we feel the weariness even more.[99]

One of the most important things I ever learned about change
is that it is always experienced as loss and always involves grief.
Mildren Tengbom is not the only one who has experienced changes
coming so thick and fast that there was not enough time to adequately process (grieve) them. We feel that loss regardless of how

---

98   Marc Lesser, *Know Yourself, Forget Yourself,* 144.
99   Mildred Tengbom, *Moving Into a New Now* (Minneapolis: Augsburg,
     1997), 48.

good the new that replaces it might be. Those of us who are seniors know the meaning of "change fatigue." We also understand:

> Accepting our changing physical reality and learning to unconditionally befriend our bodies are the major challenges at this gate. It reminds us that everything is impermanent.[100]

Just another reminder that change is inevitable.

QUESTIONS FOR REFLECTION AND CONVERSATION

1. What did you find to be most challenging in this chapter?
2. What did you find to be most helpful in this chapter?
3. What are your strategies for knowing when to accept what is and when to fight for change?

---

100 Angeles Arrien, *The Second Half of Life*, 75.

My intentions are always better than my performance.

I have probably made as many New Year's resolutions as anyone. They outlined my intentions for the coming year, and I was proud of such a commitment. It wasn't long into the new year before adjustments had to be made: I was not living up to my best intentions; I seemed unable to translate them into action. It soon became apparent that intention and action are not the same. Knowing what I want to do, what I ought to do, and what I intend to do, are not the same as making it a reality. The Sermon on the Mount ends with a crash for those who listen to Jesus' words but fail to put them into action. There are many verses that speak to the importance of our deeds (actions):

> *Let your light so shine before others, that they may see your good deeds and glorify your father in heaven* (Matthew 5:16).
> *I know your good deeds, your hard work and your perseverance* (Revelation: 2:2).
> *I know your deeds, your love and faith, your service and perseverance, and that you are now doing more than you did at first* (Revelation 2:19).
> Revelation 3:1, 8, and 15 all also contain the phrase *I know your deeds.*

Actions seem to have first place on the Divine Scorecard.

It doesn't take profound or deep exegesis to discover that God pays attention to what we do. It's the proverbial "actions speak louder than words." When it comes to judging, the only valid category for human judgments is actions. We have no idea of another's motives, desires, or intentions. We only know what they have done. God appears to favor this approach in a mostly overlooked passage to one of the seven churches:

> *Then all the churches will know that I am he who searches hearts and minds, and I will repay each of you according to your deeds* (Revelation 2:23).

Although the first chapters of Revelation are written to churches, the application applies to those members within each of the congregations. God tells them: *I will repay you according to your deeds.* It is the criterion for judgment and there is enough biblical evidence to conclude that it will be the criterion for that great final judgment when *we will all give account of ourselves to God* (Romans 14:12). This judgment is not based on what we hoped to do, intended to do, or planned to do. It dissolves into the simple, "What did we do?" It makes me aware that I'd better get busy on a plan of action for my life. I once gave my son a book titled *Action! Action! Action!* That sums up what the book was all about. Whatever our problem, dilemma, or difficulty, we much decide: "What are we going to *do* about this?"

An incremental action plan.

New Year's resolutions coupled with assembling some good intentions are not bad ideas -as long as there is an action plan to follow. I have found an action plan of achievable increments is always best and I recommend no more than three segments at a time. "I'm going to be a better person next year" is too general and lacks any place where one can gain a foothold. Although it certainly was quite a challenge in the movie *Is This as Good as it Gets?*, Jack Nicholson gives a waitress an extraordinary compliment: "You make me want to be a better man." The movie does contain some specifics on what that means for him and an action plan for ourselves must contain specifics based on shortcomings and dysfunctions we clearly see in ourselves. We have to begin with what is obvious. Specificity outlining achievable steps is more likely to bring about different actions than planning a quantum leap into near perfection.

There are always debates over whether we are what we think, we are what we feel, or we are what we do. Self-help books encourage us to think positive, helpful thoughts, to investigate our feeling and become aware of our EQ as well as our IQ. Both of these come into play in everything we do. The reasons for our actions are indeed complex. They are so many-faceted that we often find ourselves asking, "Now, why did I do that?" One of my cardinal rules which came my way years ago from a now forgotten source is: we don't feel our way into new actions, we act our way into new feelings. If we want to feel more loving, we do more loving things. If we want to feel more compassionate, we find ways to perform acts of compassion. If we want to feel more forgiving, we begin to forgive (regardless of how small our acts of forgiveness may be). "I just don't feel that way," can be countered by the question, "What might I do in order to begin to feel that way?"

The only way to judge others or ourselves.

No one but God can accurately read our motives and intentions — others can only guess at them. Anyone can see our actions. If judged solely by what we do, what kind of an evaluation would our friends (and family!) place on our lives? In Matthew 7, Jesus says the only way to tell the difference between a good tree and a bad tree is by examining the fruit. *Every good tree bears good fruit, but a bad tree bears bad fruit* (7:17). You can't see what's inside the tree but a blighted or rotten piece of fruit requires only a casual inspection. We don't know what is going on inside other people, but we can certainly ascertain what kind of people they are by their behavior and, as Jesus so clearly underscores in a sermon that is all about how to live, we are known by our actions.

MUSINGS FROM HITHER AND YON

Wisdom From another tradition.

> You are what your deep, driving desire is,
> As your desire, so is your will,
> As your will is, so is your deed,
> As your deed is, so is your destiny.
> *Brihadaranyaka Upanishad* IV.4.5

Desire to will to deed to destiny. Desire and will are driving forces in our lives but it is finally our deeds that determine our destiny. In Matthew 7:16 and 7:20 Jesus gives his prescription for recognizing a false prophet: *By their fruit you will recognize them.* The deeds tell the tale. Actions do speak volumes over words. It is finally what we do that makes the difference.

What that would call for.

> (Victor) Frankl was fond of saying that a Statue of Responsibility should be erected on the West Coast to complement the Statue of Liberty on the East.[101]

Freedom doesn't mean very much if it does not result in a responsible life of doing what contributes to making ours a better world. I have always believed in the power of words but ranting on social media is not the same as translating our concerns into actions that will help bring about the changes we want to see. David Brooks has an extended section in his book *on The Quest for a Moral Life* (sub-title) that raises all kinds of red flags about living online:

---

101 Tom Butler-Bowdon, *50 Psychology Classics*, 102.

In the age of the smartphone, the friction costs involved in making or breaking any transaction or relationship approach zero. The Internet is commanding you to click on and sample one thing after another. Living online often means living in a state of diversion. When you're living in diversion you're not actually deeply interested in things; you're just bored at a more frenetic pace. Online life is saturated with decommitment devices. If you can't focus your attention for thirty seconds, how on earth are you going to commit your life?[102]

My contention is that freedom ought to bring with it the awareness of my responsibility to make necessary commitments. Another quote from Brooks: "A life of commitment means saying a thousand noes for the sake of a few yeses."[103] The life of distraction which the Internet encourages is not the environment for being able to know when to say yes and when to say no. We simply don't have enough focus to begin to distinguish between the two.

We need to live with the daily realization that in order to become the best versions of ourselves, in order to make our small positive difference in the world, we have to focus on the deeds necessary to accomplish these goals. This is exactly the opposite of living in a state of diversion. Avoiding this diversion necessitates a commitment that enables us to get in touch with our deep, driving desire and mustering the will to perform the deeds that will bring us to the destiny we desire.

What these deeds involve our doing.

The words of Theodore Roosevelt have been quoted by many on occasions when doing what was needed involved high risk, when doing the right thing involved a real battle. Here is only a part of Roosevelt's challenge:

The credit belongs to the man who is actually in the arena, whose face is marred by dust and sweat and blood; who strives

---

102 David Brooks, *The Second Mountain*, 19.
103 Ibid, 18.

valiantly; who errs, who comes short again and again, because there is no effort with error and shortcoming; but who does actually strive to do the deeds....and who at the worst, if he fails, at least fails while daring greatly, so that his place shall never be with those cold and timid souls who neither know victory nor defeat.[104]

As I often do when a comment would only diminish what has been spoken or sung, I simply say: "Amen and amen!"

QUESTIONS FOR REFLECTION AND CONVERSATION

1. What part of this chapter spoke to you most personally?
2. Are you surprised at the repeated emphasis in Scripture on deeds and this being the basis of the final judgment?
3. How did you respond to the challenge from Theodore Roosevelt?

---

104 Matthew Kelly, *Resisting Happiness,* 179-180.

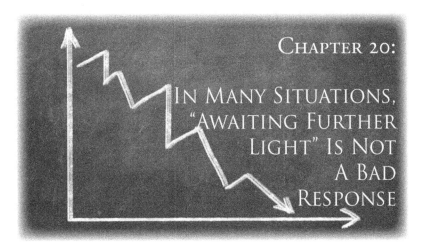

CHAPTER 20:

IN MANY SITUATIONS,
"AWAITING FURTHER
LIGHT" IS NOT
A BAD
RESPONSE

Quietness comes to the rescue.

Our Quaker friends have been especially helpful in so many areas of my spiritual life. As a person who has always seemed to be in a hurry (my mother was a living example of the biblical Martha), I needed a great deal of time for reflection and contemplation to determine what I was so busy about and why. "Awaiting further light" is some Quaker wisdom that allows time before a decision is made. To recognize there is not sufficient information on a question for a satisfactory answer, is often recognizing the need for wisdom which is not going to come from any human source. When Jesus promised that the Spirit would continue to guide us into all truth (John 16:13), he was indicating there were many things that were not accessible to human wisdom alone.

Just how much does God know that we don't know?

"Given enough time, we can work anything out" is simply not true. We continue to wrestle with issues that are as old as the first human beings and the efforts to understand themselves and their world. Many books on grief note that learning to live with unanswered questions is one of the necessities in getting on with life after a tragic loss. Isaiah 55:8 sums up a large part of the mystery of life: *"For my thoughts are not your thoughts, neither are your ways my ways," declares the Lord.* I am always taken aback when people presume to give an explanation as to why God allowed a certain thing to happen. Paul puts an even harder edge on it near the end of his carefully written theological treatise known as Romans:

> *Oh, the depth of the riches of the*
> *Wisdom and knowledge of*
> *God!*
> *How unsearchable his judgments,*
> *and his paths beyond tracing out!*
> *Who has known the mind of the Lord?*
> *Or who has been his counselor?*
> *Who has ever given to God,*
> *that God should repay them?*
> *For from him and through him and to*
> *him are all things.*
> *To him be the glory forever! Amen.* (11:33-36).

Paul must have grown weary of those who were always ready to disclose the mind of God as though they had an inside track on Divine wisdom. It's all so complex and beyond us that Paul concludes this weighty and troubling section (Romans 9-11) the way he often does when he has no clarity on a matter: he falls back on a doxology. It makes me think of either a book or chapter title I read somewhere: "Praise the Lord Anyhow!" Sometimes that is the only conclusion to which we can come as we await further light either in this world or in the world to come (see 1 Corinthians 13:12).

It's a word of caution.

"Awaiting further light" is the cautionary word to wait until there is enough light to proceed further. Perhaps we will never get the kind of illumination that makes everything perfectly clear (I have found this rarely happens), but we may have enough light to cautiously proceed ahead. Sometimes action is not the first requirement in dealing with some issue or dilemma. "Doing something is often worse than doing nothing at all." It belies the old "Don't stand there, do something!" Frequently the better advice is: "Don't do something, just stand there!" That is often the more difficult thing but the more helpful thing to do. So many tragic encounters in war resulted because of a command to go forward when there seemed like nothing else to do. If you don't really have a battle plan and don't know why you are moving forward, it seems to me best to remain in place until such a plan can be devised.

Psalm 27:14: *Wait for the Lord; be strong and take heart and wait for the Lord.* Waiting is not a strong suit for most of us. "Surely there is something we can do!" is often the response to the call to wait. Volumes have been written on the importance of timing. Doing something in the right way, for the right reason, at the right time is the proper formula for action. "It's just not the right time yet" has been the phrase that saved me from some big mistakes in ministry. These words came from the wise counsel of others who could see steps that needed to be taken before my final action plan was put into place. Most congregations, and most of us, are not ready for anything at any time. Most of us are receptive to something "whose time has come." It usually takes prayer, counsel from others, and deep searching within our souls to discover the perfect timing for something that is going to change the direction of our lives. This is not the call for a life of inactivity while we wait for some burning bush experience, but the commitment to move forward when some of the light for which have been praying breaks forth.

MUSINGS FROM HITHER AND YON

Awaiting further light requires a new openness.

If you observe people around you, you'll see that they spend ninety-nine percent of their time defending their points of view. If you just relinquish the need to defend your point of view, you will in that relinquishment, gain access to enormous amounts of energy that have previously been wasted.[105]

Constantly defending our own point of view also closes the door to new insights and may shut out the very light we need to make a better decision. It also takes a lot of energy to stay on "defense" (it also parallels football when the cry from the stands, "Defense! Defense!" means your team doesn't have the ball). Staying on the defensive will almost ensure that we won't reach our goal. Sometimes the very light we need will come from someone who has a different point of view (even a critic).

This next idea is one I believe is in harmony with Jesus' command, "Judge not" (Matthew 7):

> There is a prayer in *A Course in Miracles* that states, "Today I shall judge nothing that occurs." Non-judgment creates silence in your mind. It is a good idea, therefore, to begin your day with that statement….If practicing this procedure for the whole day seems too difficult, then you may simply say to yourself, "For the next two hours, I won't judge anything," or "For the next hour, I will experience non-judgment." Then you can extend it gradually.[106]

While not a fan of *A Course in Miracles,* I do believe this prayer suggestion would bring new insights into almost every area of our lives. We certainly live in a judgmental culture now that social media provides so much opportunity for negativity. The judgmental stance is something else that takes a lot of energy and often prevents our staying focused on the more important things in life that build relationships. Being judgmental does not create an atmosphere that encourages conversation and dialogue. The moment you speak your word of judgment you can almost see the closure on the face of the recipient. Trying the non-judgment approach couldn't hurt

---

105 105 Deepak Chopra, *The Seven Spiritual Laws of Success: A Practical Guide to the Fulfillment of Your Dreams* (San Rafael, CA: Amber-Allen Publishing, 1994), 60.

106 Ibid, 17-18.

a bit and who knows what you might discover about yourself and others in the process of your new stance?

Another term for the same principle.

> The notion of "guided drift," that we're guided by our principles but also free to embrace the flow of life, was one Fred Rogers made his own and shared with friends for the rest of his life. It strongly influenced his willingness to experiment and take chances in his career.[107]

Rogers' understanding of guided drift parallels my understanding of awaiting further light. We have our guiding principles, but we are also free to embrace the flow of life as circumstances provide new doors through which we might enter. None of these new doors is without risk, and awaiting further light never means a light that will perfectly illuminate in every way what needs to be done. Guided drift may be the best guidance for us at the time and the only way the Holy Spirit can lead us because of our present limitations.

Her faith didn't remain unraveled.

A paragraph near the end of Rachel Held Evans book *Faith Unraveled* describes faith in a fresh and challenging way gives a good place to stand while we are waiting for further light:

> What my generation is learning the hard way is that faith is not about defending conquered ground but about discovering new territory. Faith isn't about being right, or settling down, or refusing to change. Faith is a journey, and every generation contributes to its own sketches to the map. I've got miles and miles to go on this journey, but I think I can see Jesus up ahead.[108]

---

107 Maxwell King, *The Good Neighbor* (New York: Abrams Press, 2018), 118.
108 Rachel Held Evans, *Faith Unraveled*, 220.

QUESTIONS FOR REFLECTION AND CONVERSATION

1. How do you feel about the response suggested by this chapter title to the many questions and problems of our time?
2. How do you process the idea of "guided drift"?
3. Have you ever tried a non-judgmental day? What were the results?

Conclusion:
Is This As Good As It Gets?

A line to remember.

Those who have seen the 1997 movie *As Good as it Gets,* never forget Jack Nicholson's question as he walks through the waiting room of a psychiatrist's office: "What if this is as good as it gets?" This turns out to be, not only a humorous, but a perceptive and hopeful question. For the character Nicholson plays, it marks the beginning of an amazing transformation. The movie itself speaks to the possibilities that lie hidden under so much of life's hurt, pain, and rubble. The transformation spills over into the lives of a family that was living with a full bucket of impossibilities. If you summarize the moral of the movie it is simply: No, this is not as good as it can get if we are willing to listen and act and change.

I put this question into a larger frame and ask if this life on earth with all of its chaos, confusion, warfare, hostility, and evil is God's last word for his creation? A vast host, both past and present, have agreed that this isn't as good as it's going to get. The Bible is really a library of books with two great bookends: Genesis with its — I*n the beginning God created* and Revelation with its — *Then I saw a new heaven and a new earth* (21:1). The description in Revelation 21 is of the kind of world all of us have longed for and dreamed about — where tears are wiped away, death is no more, and God actively dwells and lives with his people in the restored

Garden of Eden transformed into something far better. It is a place of life, and blessing, and harmony, and opportunity, and possibility unmarred by the onslaughts of evil in any form. It is life the way God intended from the very beginning.

We've only been given the big picture.

A major fault I find with too many people who believe in a life to come after this one is that they want to insert too many specifics. The Bible is short on specifics but long on the assurance that God will provide such a life in his second great act of creation. John 14 gives this picture of what is to be expected: it is a place the Father will provide and it will have plenty of room for all of his children. The classic King James Translation quotes Jesus as saying, *"In my Father's house are many mansions...."* Better translations render this: *"In my Father's house are many dwelling places."* Some see this as a downgrade in accommodations! I guarantee than any *dwelling place* in the celestial city will not be a disappointment. And I don't believe God has some budget bungalows for those who just get in by the skin of their teeth. I cannot imagine anything less heavenly than "merit" subdivisions where rank and privilege are the order of the day. That is this world, not the world to come! As the ground is level at the foot of the cross, so I believe the ground to be level in God's perfect Kingdom.

C. S. Lewis is frequently cited for his take on the next life. He confesses that he really doesn't have any accurate descriptions, but he is convinced that it a place that will be like an exciting novel, where each new chapter is better than the one before. I cannot imagine any better way to pen the answer to the question, "Is this as good as it gets?"

MUSINGS FROM HITHER AND YON

The question many of us ask.

> How could life be almost over, we worry, when we were just beginning to understand it, to enjoy it, to love it?[109]

That feeling and that question have come to me and many other seniors with whom I have had serious discussions about reaching the "twilight" of life. It certainly doesn't seem fair that about the time we are beginning to understand so much more about ourselves and about life the curtain is about to come down.

The Gospel of Mark is almost universally believed to be the first of the Gospels. Its favorite word, *immediately*, takes us on a breath-taking excursion through the most extraordinary life ever lived. There are many indications in the writing that we are reading an eyewitness account with many small details the other Gospel writings omit. What seems most authenticating about the reality of the account is the way the Gospel ends. When the women come to the tomb on a Sunday morning to anoint Jesus' body for proper burial, the only question they have is, "Who will roll away the stone?" None of the women, singularly or in concert, have the strength to move the heavy rock from the mouth of the burial cave. When they arrive at the site, their question is irrelevant — the stone has already been taken away. When they enter the tomb, they do not encounter a dead body but *a young man dressed in a white robe sitting on the right side* (Mark 16:5). The text tells us *they were alarmed* but what they heard from the young man was even more alarming:

> *You are looking for Jesus of Nazareth, who was crucified. He has risen! He is not here. See the place where they laid him. But go, tell his disciples and Peter, "He is going ahead of you into Galilee. There you will see him, just as he told you"* (Mark 16:6-7).

---

109 Joan Chittister, *The Gift of Years* (New York: BlueBridge, 2008), 41.

You would think the Bible would present the women as shouting for joy and leaving the tomb with "Hallelujahs" over the unbelievable good news. Instead, we have what most would consider a natural, all too human, response to such a vision and announcement. Mark tells us: *Trembling and bewildered, the women went out and fled from the tomb.*

The original ending of Mark is a real cliffhanger. Almost all scholars agree that verses nine through twenty of Chapter 16 are later additions by other persons who couldn't live with an unfinished Gospel. But I'm convinced it is finished with the end of verse eight.

> When Mark leaves us with *"gar"* (a Greek proposition) at the end of verse 8, Mark frustrates the desire for a formal ending that we bring with us to the narrative. A literal translation: "They said nothing to anyone, they were afraid for...." — leaves us hanging.[110]

As many have said before me: we are left to finish the story in the Galilees of our own lives.

It's never been said better.

> The best thing I've heard lately is the Christian writer Barbara Johnson's saying that we're Easter people, living in a Good Friday world.[111]

This did not originate with Barbara Johnson but I am at a loss to remember where I first heard it. It has been echoed in countless sermons and I have used it in numerous Easter messages. The reason I like Mark's ending is that it keeps us living in a Good Friday world even though we now have become Easter people. In the light of our present condition, John Hick raises what he terms the ultimate question:

---

110 John Ortberg, *God is Closer Than You Think* (Grand Rapids: Zondervan, 2005), 100.
111 Anne Lamott, *Plan B,* 140.

I therefore end by formulating this ultimate question which lies at the heart of the theodicy problem: can there be a future good so great as to render acceptable, in retrospect, the whole human experience, with all its wickedness and suffering as well as all its sanctity and happiness? I think that perhaps there can, and indeed that perhaps there is.[112]

I would only make one change in that paragraph: I would strike the word *perhaps* to make the last sentence read: I think that perhaps there can, and indeed there is.

A final message from a cemetery.

(It involves) the resting place of Mel Blanc, the famous voice of countless characters in *Looney Tunes*. In accordance with his instructions, his family inscribed as his final epitaph the words he had said to end a thousand cartoons: *"That's all folks."* Philip Yancey tells about the grave of a friend's grandmother who lies buried under ancient oak trees in the cemetery of an Episcopal church in rural Louisiana. In accordance with the grandmother's instructions, only one word is inscribed on the tombstone: *Waiting.*[113]

Mel Blanc's epitaph was for a different reason in a different context. The grandmother's epitaph speaks for all of us who are Easter people living in a Good Friday world. One day that Easter will belong to us in all of its fullness.

QUESTIONS FOR REFLECTION AND CONVERSATION

1. What do you think about the interpretation Mark as given in this conclusion?
2. Why do you believe we have not been given many specifics about the life to come?

---

112 John Hick, *Evil and the Love of God* (New York: Harper & Row, 1977), 386.
113 John Ortberg, *Who Is This Man?* (Grand Rapids: Zondervan, 2012), 196.

3. Do you feel C.S. Lewis's comparison of the next life to a novel, answers the title question of this Conclusion in a broader context?

Altman, Donald. *Clearing Emotional Clutter.* New York: MJF Books, 2016.

Arrien, Angeles. *The Second Half of Life.* Boulder: Sounds True, 2005.

Brooks, David. *The Second Mountain: The Quest for a Moral Life.* New York: Random House, 2019.

Brueggemann, Walter. *An Unsettling God.* Minneapolis: Fortress Press, 2009.

Buechner, Frederick. *Listening to Your Life.* New York: HarperSan Francisco, 1992.

Butler-Bowdon, Tom. *50 Psychology Classics: Who We Are, How We Think, What We Do.* London: Nicholas Brealey Publishing, 2003.

———. *50 Self-Help Classics: 50 Inspirational Books to Transform Your Life.* New York: MJF Books, 2007.

Campbell, Will. *Soul Among Lions.* Louisville: John Knox Press, 1999.

Chittister, Joan. *The Gift of Years.* New York: BlueBridge, 2008.

———. *The Way We Were.* New York: Orbis Books, 2005.

Chopra, Deepak. *The Seven Spiritual Laws of Success: A Practical Guide for the Fulfillment of Your Dreams.* San Rafael, CA: Amber-Allen Publishing, 1994.

Ellsberg, Robert. *The Saints' Guide to Happiness.* New York: North Point Press, 2003.

Evans, Rachel Held. *Faith Unraveled: How a Girl Who Knew All the Answers Learned to Ask Questions.* Grand Rapids: Zondervan, 2010.

Fox, Michael J. *Always Looking Up: The Adventures of an Incurable Optimist.* New York: Hyperion, 2009.

Gaddy, Welton. *A Soul Under Siege.* Louisville: Westminster/John Knox Press, 1991.

Geisler, Norman. *If God Why Evil?* Minneapolis: Bethany House, 2011.

Godsey, Kirby. *The Courage Factor: A Collection of Presidential Essays.* Macon: Mercer University Press, 2005.

Hall, Christopher A. and Sanders, John. *Does God Have a Future: A Debate on Divine Providence.* Grand Rapids: Baker Academic, 2003.

Hick, John. *Evil and the Love of God.* New York: Harper & Row, 1977.

Hilton, James. *Lost Horizon.* Cleveland: World Publishing, 1936.

Huston, Paula. *Forgiveness.* Brewster: Paraclete Press, 2008.

Kelly, Matthew. *The Biggest Lie in the History of Christianity.* Kakadu, Australia, no publisher listed, 2018.

_____. *Perfectly Yourself.* New York: Ballantine Books, 2006.

_____. *Resisting Happiness.* Erlanger, KY: Beacon Publishing, 2016.

King, Maxwell. *The Good Neighbor.* New York: Abrams Press, 2018.

Kreamer, Anne. *It's Always Something*. New York: Random House, 2011.

Lamott, Anne. *Plan B: Further Thoughts on Faith*. New York: Riverhead Books, 2005.

Lesser, Marc. *Know Yourself, Forget Yourself*. New York: New World Library, 2013.

Levine, Amy-Jill and Brettler, Marc Zvi, eds. *The Jewish Annotated New Testament*. New York: Oxford University Press, 1911.

Lightner, Candy and Hathaway, Nancy. *Giving Sorrow Words*. New York: Warner Books, 1990.

Limburg, James. *Encountering Ecclesiastes: A Book for Our Time*. Grand Rapids: William B. Eerdmans, 2008.

Manning, Brennan. *All is Grace*. Colorado Springs: David C. Cook, 2011.

_____. *The Ragamuffin Gospel*. Sisters, OR: Multnomah Publishers, 2000.

Martin, James. *Between Heaven and Mirth*. New York: HarperOne, 2011.

_____. *The Jesuit Guide to Almost Everything: A Spirituality for Real Life*. New York: HarperOne, 2010.

McGraw Phillip. *Life Strategies*. New York: Hyperion, 1999.

Ortberg, John. *God is Closer Than You Think*. Grand Rapids: Zondervan, 2005.

_____. *Who Is This Man?* Grand Rapids: Zondervan, 2012.

Palmer, Parker J. *To Know As We Are Known*. New York: HarperSanFrancisco, 1993.

Peck, M. Scott. *An Anthology of Wisdom*. Kansas City: Ariel Books, 1996.

Poole, Charles E. *The Tug of Home*. Macon: Peake Road, 1997.

Powell, Tia. *Dementia Reimagined: Building a Life of Joy and Dignity From Beginning to End*. New York: Avery, 2019.

Rohr, Richard. *Falling Upward: A Spirituality for the Two Halves of Life.* San Francisco: Jossey-Bass, 2011.

_____. *The Naked Now: Learning to See as the Mystics See.* New York: Crossroad Publishing, 2009.

Sapolsky, Robert M. *Behave: The Biology of Humans at our Best and Worst.* New York: Penguin Books, 2017.

Singer, Michael. *The Untethered Soul.* Oakland, CA: New Harbinger Publications, 2007.

Tengbom, Mildred. *Moving Into a New Now.* Minneapolis: Augsburg, 1997.

Thielicke, Helmut. *Living With Death.* Grand Rapids: William B. Eerdmans, 1983.

Yaconelli, Michael. *Messy Spirituality.* Grand Rapids: Zondervan, 2002.

Yancey, Phillip. *What's So Amazing About Grace?* Grand Rapids: Zondervan Publishing, 1997.

Walsch, Neale Donald. *When Everything Changes Change Everything.* Ashland, OR: EmNin Books, 2009.

Waters, Larry J. and Zuck, Roy B., eds. *Why, O God?: Suffering and Disability in the Bible and Church.* Wheaton: Crossway, 2011.

Wicks, Robert. *After 50.* New York: Paulist Press, 1997.

Wilkes, Paul. *Beyond the Walls.* New York: Image Books, 1999.

ALSO FROM ENERGION PUBLICATIONS

Brings the good news that discussions about aging can bring new purpose, meaning, and hope to all of life — regardless of your present age.

BY RON HIGDON

Blending biblical and conventional wisdom with relevant stories and experiences has produced a superb guide toward a healthy ministry and church.

Bill Wilson
Director, The Center for Healthy Churches

More from Energion Publications

Personal Study

Holy Smoke! Unholy Fire	Bob McKibben	$14.99
The Jesus Paradigm	David Alan Black	$17.99
When People Speak for God	Henry Neufeld	$17.99
The Jesus Manifesto	David Moffett-Moore	$9.99

Christian Living

Faith in the Public Square	Robert D. Cornwall	$16.99
Grief: Finding the Candle of Light	Jody Neufeld	$8.99
Crossing the Street	Robert LaRochelle	$16.99
Surviving a Son's Suicide	Ron Higdon	$9.99

Bible Study

Learning and Living Scripture	Lentz/Neufeld	$12.99
Those Footnotes in Your New Testament	Thomas W. Hudgins	$5.99
Luke: A Participatory Study Guide	Geoffrey Lentz	$8.99
Philippians: A Participatory Study Guide	Bruce Epperly	$9.99
Ephesians: A Participatory Study Guide	Robert D. Cornwall	$9.99

Theology

Creation in Scripture	Herold Weiss	$12.99
Creation: the Christian Doctrine	Edward W. H. Vick	$12.99
The Politics of Witness	Allan R. Bevere	$9.99
Ultimate Allegiance	Robert D. Cornwall	$9.99
History and Christian Faith	Edward W. H. Vick	$9.99
The Church Under the Cross	William Powell Tuck	$11.99
The Journey to the Undiscovered Country	William Powell Tuck	$9.99
Eschatology: A Participatory Study Guide	Edward W. H. Vick	$9.99

Ministry

Clergy Table Talk	Kent Ira Groff	$9.99
Out of the Office: A Theology of Ministry	Robert D. Cornwall	$9.99

Generous Quantity Discounts Available
Dealer Inquiries Welcome
Energion Publications — P.O. Box 841
Gonzalez, FL_ 32560
Website: http://energionpubs.com
Phone: (850) 525-3916

CPSIA information can be obtained
at www.ICGtesting.com
Printed in the USA
FSHW010225010520
69795FS